When Did You Know...

When Did You Know...

~

He Was Not The One?

JUDY BOLTON
AND
WENDY BOLTON FLOYD

iUniverse, Inc.
New York Lincoln Shanghai

When Did You Know ...
He Was Not The One?

iUniverse books may be ordered through booksellers or by contacting:

iUniverse
2021 Pine Lake Road, Suite 100
Lincoln, NE 68512
www.iuniverse.com
1-800-Authors (1-800-288-4677)

The information, ideas, and suggestions in this book are not intended as a substitute for professional advice. Neither the authors nor the publisher shall be liable or responsible for any loss or damage allegedly arising as a consequence of your use or application of any information or suggestions in this book. Names have been changed.

ISBN-13: 978-0-595-41146-7 (pbk)
ISBN-13: 978-0-595-85504-9 (ebk)
ISBN-10: 0-595-41146-0 (pbk)
ISBN-10: 0-595-85504-0 (ebk)

Printed in the United States of America

In loving memory of our grandmother Arnietta Butler

For our parents, Joseph and Yvonne Bolton, for believing in us and offering support. We love you.
—JB and WBF

ACKNOWLEDGMENTS

On a personal note, thanks to my wonderful sons, Christopher and Jordan. You are so wonderful and supportive. I will love you forever. I would like to acknowledge the local takeout restaurants—Gino's, Imperial Wok, McDonald's—that ensured that my sons and I were fed when I was too busy to cook. Thanks to those moms whose children appeared on Sesame Street with my son. Many a day I asked "When did you know he was not the one?" as we sat together in the green room. I got the idea for this book from those lively discussions.
—JB

My personal thanks go to first and foremost, my husband and best friend, Gregory, a man I can always count on. You supported me and managed our household for several months as this book was being written. And to our beautiful children Jessica and Jonathan. I love you all dearly. Also thank you to the following people for always responding to me with complete honesty: Cheryl Wills; John Singleton; Stephanie Smith Clarke; Dane Clarke; Crystal Wills and Sherria Seward. Sincere thanks to Chris Gardner for taking Greg and I out to dinner one rainy evening and encouraging me to pursue "happyness" in writing this book! Your assistance and advice throughout this process has been invaluable.
—WBF

This book could not have been written without the candor of the forty-one women who shared their stories with us. This book is a celebration of their wisdom, courage, honesty and their remarkable zest for life.

We want to offer our thanks to Susan Driscoll, CEO of iUniverse Publishing, for seeing the potential in this project right from the start; Marna Poole, our editor extraordinaire, for tweaking the stories and Randolph Smith, our dearest friend, for being our sounding board throughout this entire project and always offering helpful advice.

We also are most appreciative of the services of our incredible production team: Lenni Adelman (Wantagh Business Services), our invaluable transcriber, who spent many hours toiling over our material; Darryl Harrison, our talented and patient cameraman and producer; Ronnie Wright, photographer to the stars; Dorothy Shi and Kenson Noel, talented photographers; our hair stylist Michaella Blissett-Williams; our fashion stylist and make-up artist, Rahel Berihu. Kirsten Hemming at eggscollective.org, for designing our phenomenal website; Eugenia "Jean" Woody, for getting the word out to the Women's Media Center, and other valuable media outlets; and Amy Bodden, for introducing us to the wonderful world of blogging. We would especially like to thank the Barrau family for graciously allowing us to shoot When Did You Know ... promos in their home.

Special thanks to Rachael Ray and Meredith Weinstein, producer of the Rachael Ray show; Yahoo! Personals and Jason Khoury, and the PR team (especially Susan Bean) at Fleishman-Hillard. Thanks also to Sarah Langbein, of the Orlando Sentinel; WWOR Radio; Meredith Wagner, Executive Vice President; Geralyn Lucas, Director of Programming; and especially Claire Hambrick of Lifetime

Television. We also offer thanks to Carolyn Nurnberg, Associate Vice President of Rubenstein Communications, Inc. and Patricia Maffei of The Fashion Group International.

Our thanks also go to Clarins for sponsoring our Whine and Cheese events and the wonderful and talented Clarins staff—Tanya Pushkine Rojas; Christine Tedesco; Chantal Sanders; Nicole Matusow; Tranda Misini; Joseph McElroy; Loretta Smith and Megan Dennen and to Ritchie and Joyce Calcasola at Maximus Salon & Spa and their amazing and dedicated staff.

And we especially appreciate the participation of the following organizations in the creation of this book: Parents Without Partners, Visions Anew, the National Association of Female Executives (NAFE), Women's Networking Group of Long Island, Girl Scouts of the USA, The Fashion Group Inc., the National Association of Women Business Owners, and the Women Business Owners Network of Vermont.

—JB and WBF

CONTENTS

INTRODUCTION

~

When Did You Know … He Was Not the One? was conceived at a time when I was contemplating a divorce, which, coincidentally, was the same time that my sister, Wendy, was planning her wedding. Even though Wendy seemed blissful, I had become skeptical about the concept of marriage—not surprising, given my situation at the time—and so I began soliciting the opinions of other married women, just to see if I was the lone passenger on this particular lifeboat. Were most married women actually happy, or were they as disenchanted, disappointed, and dissatisfied as I was? Maybe, I conjectured, there was a large group of women who were masking their inner feelings about their mates. Could it be, I wondered, that women were so desperate that they would tolerate and remain in dysfunctional relationships?

I spoke with several friends and quickly discovered that most of them were unhappy in their relationships; not only that, each woman could pinpoint the exact moment when she realized that the man she had chosen was not "the one."

Bride-to-be Wendy, ever game for a good story, made her own observations. Even though she was sure that she *had* found "the one," she spoke with friends who were less than thrilled with their own choices. Wendy discovered, as I had, that many of those women could recall the "light bulb" moment when they realized that there was nothing more they could do to salvage their relationships.

Although all the women seemed united in their shared sense of a defining moment, we quickly realized that the moment was different for each woman. And we decided that it would be interesting to learn just how many different "moments" there were, by gathering that information from women across the country.

The women who have shared their stories in this book come from varied backgrounds. Some are housewives; some are business executives. Many have traveled extensively; a few have never seen much of the world beyond their own backyards. Some finished their education when they graduated from high school; others went on to become doctors or attorneys. What binds these women, however, is the suffering they endured as their relationships floundered.

The women we interviewed expressed themselves vividly and colorfully, so much so that Wendy and I felt as if we were in "the moment" with them; we could feel a range of emotions emanating from these warm, bright, and intuitive women. For several of the women, it was the first time they had told their stories, and that was cathartic for them, as well as empowering. We all shared many tears—and a great deal of laughter.

Over the course of our research, one point stood out with crystal clarity: Too many women make serious mistakes when they decide with whom to spend the rest of their lives; they seem to choose the wrong mate for the wrong reasons.

An overwhelming number of the women we interviewed thought they could "change" their partners once they were settled into their relationship. Perhaps predictably, the behavior they hoped to change only intensified as the relationship progressed.

It also became clear to us that many women jumped into sexual involvement too quickly. Sexual involvement tends to cloud one's mind, and a clouded mind is not inclined to make good decisions.

Other women spent too little time in really getting to know their future mates. There was no sense of emotional safety with their mates, no calmness or peace in their relationships. Often, the women were unable to fully express themselves and lacked a sense of self-worth.

When Did You Know ... He Was Not the One? should not be viewed as a "how-to" book—obviously, women and men can live together in delightful harmony (Wendy and her husband are a strong case in point). Still, for those women who are silently suffering in an impossible relationship, we hope this book will be a comfort. We hope they will realize that they are not doomed to stand on the deck of the *Titanic* as the last lifeboat is lowered without them. And we hope that this collection of stories will provide them with courage and strength and that it will propel them to take positive action to improve their lives.

MOIRA

~

At sixty-two years old, Moira has learned to make her words count. Although she can speak five languages, her voice was all but silenced during her marriage. She grew up as the daughter of a linguist, who, ironically, wasn't terribly interested in anything Moira had to say; her husband later repeated this pattern. Now divorced, Moira is the owner of a flourishing flower shop in the suburbs of St. Paul, Minnesota.

I was married for thirty-nine years to a man who was not the right one for me. I recognized that sad fact early on, but I stayed in the marriage for the sake of our four children. I suppose I learned that ethic from my mother.

My mother was barely twenty years old when she married my father, who was twenty-one at that time. My parents were Irish, but they grew up in England, as did I. I think my parents had tremendous affection for each other, but my father's family history—his parents divorced when he was quite young—prevented him from understanding how to treat women appropriately. In fact, I believe he actually was quite afraid of women. He was raised by his mother and grandmother, both of whom were strict and forbidding.

My mother also grew up in a women-dominated environment, as she was sent to a convent boarding school from the time she was eight years old until she was sixteen. She was beautiful, but she had little experience with men when she met my father.

My father was a selfish man, and his seeming inability to consider my mother's feelings had a strong impact on my parents' relationship. My father worked as a flight engineer for a major commercial airline, and because he was quite good-looking, he received lots of attention from the female flight attendants. He reciprocated their attention, as he was a bit of a flirt, even though he secretly feared women.

My mother was in the women's Navy during World War II, which is when she became pregnant with me. She was given something to induce abortion because she was needed in the war effort and a pregnancy would have made her unavailable. Obviously, the medication didn't work, but I think my father wished that it had—he was angry that his first born was a girl. My sister was born six years later, and my father was disappointed once again. When my mother finally presented my father with a son, three years after my sister's birth, both my parents were thrilled—even though my father eventually became jealous of the attention my mother gave to my brother. I don't know if this jealousy played any part in my father's extramarital activities, but I do know with certainty that all during my parents' marriage, my father had affairs. I also believe that my mother was aware of these liaisons but chose to ignore them.

Because of his job, which allowed him to stay in hotels in exotic parts of the world, my father enjoyed a playboy lifestyle. I do think, though, that he was frustrated and angry with himself, because he was essentially living a double life. He was traveling all over the world, acting the part of the playboy, but then he would come home and have to be a husband and father.

Throughout my childhood, my father's job kept him away from home for three weeks at a time; then he'd be home for one week. It was during that one week that he gave out punishments, as he always was convinced that I had misbehaved while he was away. My mother never stood up for me, nor did she try to soothe me after my father had unjustly punished me.

After years of living this way, I looked for an escape; I thought marriage would be my way out. It was difficult for me, though, because I did not have a good model for a loving relationship. Based on life in my household, as I was growing up, love looked pretty awful to me.

I met Tony in January 1964 while I was working as a ground assistant. I was a VIP hostess for the airlines. I was responsible for the VIP lounge and looked after all the dignitaries. He was in the United States Air Force, stationed in England. I was only nineteen years old at the time and quite naïve, so when Tony asked for my phone number, I gave it to him. Tony was twenty-five years old, tall, and extremely handsome. We quickly discovered that we were both Catholic—an important point, because at the time, it was assumed that if a couple had a common religion, everything else would be okay. Tony was first-generation Italian, a fact, I later realized, that meant his attitude toward women was much like my father's—he needed women but was terrified of them, and therefore, tried to berate them.

I was extremely attracted to Tony, and once we started dating, I saw no one else. It was not, however, the same for Tony. Throughout our courtship, he had sex with other women. Oddly, he didn't see this as a problem, but it was a definite red flag for me; it made me realize, very early on, that he was not "the one." Still, even though I knew there were other women, I justified Tony's behavior by convincing myself that he was unfaithful only because he and I were not having sex. And I fooled myself into thinking that once we were engaged, he would be true to me. Of course, this was not the case. In fact, I caught him with a woman in his apartment. But even then, my only response was to walk out and go home. Tony didn't even bother to follow me to explain. Eventually, catching him with other women became a pattern for us; after he got caught, he would simply call me and invite me for dinner the next day. I would accept—and we would go on as though nothing had happened.

I refused to acknowledge that his infidelities were a problem, because Tony was my ticket out of my parents' household. I had a wonderful life with the airlines, and that job had enabled me to receive a creditable amount of attention. I was on television, I was in films, I did all sorts of amazingly visible things. But I always felt as though I lived on a small island. I always thought there must be somewhere else to go. I remember dating the son of a German doctor and considering leaving England and moving to Germany with that man, even though I didn't love him. I was so eager to escape from my household that I think a part of me had a wanderlust. Marrying Tony would provide me the opportunity to escape. He was very handsome, and in spite of being sexually active with other women, he could be extremely kind, and I was incredibility attracted to him.

Although my mother warned me against marrying Tony, I believed that once we were married, he would become completely faithful to me—even though some part of me realized that I would be swimming upstream the whole time. When our wedding day arrived, and I looked down the aisle to see Tony standing at the altar, I remember thinking, "I haven't a clue who this man is." Still, I felt extraordinary pressure to continue on with the wedding—one hundred people from all over the world were waiting for me. And so we were married, and Tony pledged to love and cherish me. He recited his vows as though he meant them.

We made love for the first time on the night of our wedding. All I can remember about it now is that I felt extremely disappointed by it. We honeymooned in Europe and went to Tony's family home on the Adriatic Sea. This, too, was a difficult experience, as his family wanted Tony to spend all his time with them—on *our* honeymoon!

We did manage to have some time alone, though—I conceived our first child while we were in Europe.

After our honeymoon, we settled into life in England. At that time, wives of Air Force officers were not permitted to have outside jobs. This was all right with me; although I'd loved my career, I wanted to be a wife and mother. I wanted to bring up our children in a loving, two-parent environment. I viewed my marriage as my opportunity to create something I'd never experienced. It didn't take long, however, for that bubble to burst. My pregnancy caused awful morning sickness, but Tony did not offer any support or sympathy—he was too busy entertaining his friends to be bothered with caring for his pregnant wife. This was when I had to accept that Tony exhibited a coldness toward me; all of his warmth and charisma was offered to everyone else. He had nothing for me.

Our first child—a son—was born in April. This happy occasion was saddened by news that my great-grandmother had taken ill and was dying. Also at this time, Tony received word that he had been accepted into the PhD program at Minnesota State University—we were to move to the United States within six weeks. And it was up to me—with a new baby, a dying grandmother, and ambivalence about leaving England—to prepare our home for the military white-glove inspection that would take place before our departure. My hormones were all over the chart, and Tony was not emotionally present.

From the start, our life in Mankato, Minnesota, was difficult for me. Tony insisted that I did not need to get an American driver's license because, he said, he would drive me to wherever I needed to go—that effectively isolated me at home. It was probably my naiveté, but I did everything on Tony's terms. I suppose part of the reason for my acquiescence was because I was in a new country with a small baby, and I had to trust Tony to take care of us. For his part, Tony seemed ashamed that he was married to an "immigrant"; he feared that people would think less of him because of it. He also became very controlling of our finances. Even though the Air Force was paying for all of our expenses while Tony was in school, I was on a very tight budget. Tony's generosity extended only to his friends, for whom he spared no expense. I felt controlled and trapped, and Tony was unsupportive. As long as his own needs were met, he didn't consider mine. His selfishness soon became even more apparent to me, due to an embarrassing incident. Tony was swamped with school work and often studied late into the night. On one of those nights, I put on a black picture hat and high heels—and nothing else. Then I went to his office, draped myself provocatively against the door frame, and asked Tony if there was anything that I could get for him. He looked at me for a few seconds, said "No, thanks," and went back to his books. I was completely devastated! This incident was a clear indication that something was wrong in our relationship. I had never felt so rejected in my entire life.

Over the next few years, Tony's career really took off, while I was busy having babies. Although I was very committed to being Mummy, I was extremely lonely and felt very isolated. Tony had very little to say to me, and I hadn't made any friends in Minnesota. I spent most of my free time writing letters to my mother in England.

When Tony graduated in 1969, I was sure he would now direct his focus to being a husband and a father. We relocated to Phoenix, Arizona, which I fell in love with immediately, and I had high hopes that life would be good for us. But within one month, Tony received notice that he would be stationed in Korea for thirteen months, and he would have to go without me or our sons. Initially, I was scared, but the separation turned out to be the most brilliant thing that ever happened in our marriage. While Tony was away, I had total autonomy. I took care of everything, and I was in control of my life. I controlled our finances; I got my driver's license, and I met lots of people who became friends.

When people ask me about the happiest point in my marriage, I usually respond that it was the year that Tony was away. Yet it's funny how life works, because six months after Tony left for Korea, I began to miss him and decided that I would go to Korea to surprise him.

Tony was thrilled by my surprise arrival, and I began to see a ray of hope for the first time in our marriage. Still, I realized that when he returned home, my newly acquired independence would not be well received by him.

For now, though, I was happy—and I returned to the States with a souvenir from my trip to Korea: I was pregnant. It was an easy time for me, without any trace of morning sickness. My neighbors and friends were amazing, and I developed tremendous friendships during that year. I was enjoying life—and then, six months into my pregnancy, Tony returned.

We soon learned that he was to be stationed in England again, and although I was returning to my homeland, I knew that this promotion for Tony meant that he would be working even longer hours than he had been.

My marriage was very lonely, and I didn't know how to fix it. When I tried to explain to Tony how I was feeling, he would respond that he was "providing." It was true that we lived in the beautiful, upscale General Quarters, and the children attended a private school. Our life looked great on the outside, but on the inside, it was very cold; most of the time, the children and I were alone at home. It seemed that the only time Tony noticed me was when he wanted sex. It shouldn't be surprising, then, that I became pregnant again.

Quite often, I was expected to prepare gourmet dinners for Tony's colleagues from work. He would call at the last minute to let me know that he was bringing someone home for dinner, and I was expected to whip up a fabulous meal. I hated it; I hated the pressure of providing meals and looking perfect all the time. I was providing comfort to my husband through food, much as his mother had done, but Tony provided me only with a place to live. I received no true comfort from him; there was no sign that he even thought about me.

Later in our marriage, we began to have sex on demand—his demand. I told him, years later, that I accepted sex from him just so I could be held. I wanted some kind of touching, some kind of comfort. And so I would agree to sex, just to have that need fulfilled. Of course my sexual needs were never fulfilled; it wasn't important to Tony whether or not I was satisfied. He was a selfish lover.

We returned to the States in 1976. I was apprehensive about returning, because once again, Tony had been promoted, and I knew the amount of his neglect was likely to increase. At this point in our marriage, I was not under any delusions. I found, though, that by having a drink in the evening, I could dull the pain. Eventually, however, my solitary drinking reached a point where I agreed to attend Alcoholics Anonymous (AA) meetings. I followed a twelve-step program at AA for thirteen years, and it actually became my social life. I met the most amazing wonderful people, and I learned how to be strong and stand up for myself. Although I didn't see myself as an alcoholic, I enjoyed the meetings, where I would receive approval and encouragement from others in the group. It was the type of encouragement that I was unable to get from my husband. For the first time in my adult life, I was surrounded by people who had compassion and who cared about me. And because of their support, I was able to spread my wings and grow into the woman I am today. This growth, however, made Tony very, very uncomfortable. He wanted me to remain completely dependent on him; he had to have all the control.

Our relationship continued to deteriorate, but I never suspected that Tony would try to end it. Two years before I would ultimately make up my mind to leave him, he woke me at five-thirty to tell me that our marriage was over, that he could no longer live with me. I was suddenly wide awake. I bolted straight up in bed and said, "Well, it's about bloody time that you acknowledge there is something wrong in our marriage!" I then asked him what he was planning to do. Was he calling it quits, I asked, or did he want to do something to make it better? He got up without another word, and he never mentioned it again—at least, not until another morning, about a year later. He woke me up at five in the morning, as if it were some kind of anniversary. And he repeated the words he'd said the year before: that our marriage wasn't working and that he could no longer live with me. And once again, after the words were out of his mouth, he ignored and denied he had ever said them.

Two years later—we had been married for thirty-six years at the time—we were attending Tony's retirement ceremony. It seemed that everyone who had ever worked with him was present, and they all were in awe of him. When Tony made his speech, he mentioned that he planned to enjoy his retirement. He wanted to spend time traveling, hiking, and doing all the things he'd not had time for while working. *And that was my defining moment, because his speech did not include any reference to me. He didn't thank me for my support during his career; he didn't acknowledge the many dinners I'd prepared for his colleagues; he made no note of my tireless effort to be a good wife. I was totally unacknowledged—pretty much the way I had been unacknowledged throughout our entire marriage.*

I'd always accepted the sacrifices I'd made in our marriage because I honestly thought that one day, Tony would turn to me and say, "Okay, honey, now it's our turn." I also thought that by staying in the marriage, I was being a good mother—I couldn't cause the break up of my children's home. Our family had grown to three very active young boys and a daughter, and I could not envision being a single parent. But as I sat at this ceremony, I realized that my children were the cement in my marriage; there was no mutual love between my husband and me. The children were what had kept us together.

So it was at that precise moment that I realized I would never be a priority in Tony's life. And I decided that I wanted a different life; I decided that I was going to leave Tony.

Two days later, I got a call about a house that was about to be put up for rent, so I went out to see it. The house was located on a bluff overlooking the city—a beautiful setting—and as I walked across the threshold, I became so overwhelmed that I burst into tears—I knew I had found my refuge. The gentleman who owned the home greeted me by putting his arms around me. "Come sit down, Moira," he said. "I think you're home."

I left my marriage several months later. Tony was in Italy, visiting his family, and while he was away, I packed everything in our house and left. When I picked up Tony at the airport, I explained that when he got home, he'd find that I no longer lived there. He responded by inviting me in for a cup of tea. That's just how calm he was. Clearly, my announcement had no emotional effect on him. As always, he thought only of himself.

Now, three years after the divorce, I've come to realize that Tony couldn't see me for who I was; he never tried. I know I was the best I could be for him—although he never acknowledged or appreciated it—but now, I'm just the best I am for me.

When I was a little girl, my grandfather often took me to the beach. My mother had always kept my hair braided, but on my walks with my grandfather, he would undo my braids and let my hair go free. I'd run up and down on the beach, my hair flying in the wind. One time, I ran to the edge of the tide, where the water was just stopping, and put my head down on the sand. My grandfather said, "Get up, you silly girl! You'll get your hair wet."

"But Grandfather," I replied, "I'm listening to the heartbeat of the world."

A close friend observed that I was able to withstand the pain in my marriage because I had not brought that little girl with me into my adult life; somehow, I was smart enough to leave her behind. Recently, however, I made a concerted effort to find her again. I went back to the little beach in England where I'd pressed my cheek against the sand, and I picked up a little pebble, right where I thought I left it as a child. That pebble now sits on a little table, surrounded by silver and gold filigree. It's a beautiful stone that catches the sunlight in its special spot, and it serves to remind me that although my inner child was deeply wounded, she was also extraordinarily strong.

At age sixty-two, I have been able to recapture my playful spirit, and I do all kinds of fun things. I ride horses and motorcycles; I host parties and take gourmet cooking classes. I no longer live with pretense or illusion. I am living authentically. I am authentically me.

NANCY

~

Fifty-one-year-old Nancy is twice divorced. She married for the first time while still in her teens to escape a difficult home life, and she married her second husband just a few months after divorcing the first. Since her second marriage ended, Nancy has learned to be her own woman. She knows that she doesn't have to be with a man to define herself, and she is no longer afraid to live on her own. Nancy is employed as a supervisor in a juvenile detention center in Springfield, Illinois.

---

*M*y parents were divorced shortly after my first birthday. My mom remarried when I was four years old, but it was hell for me. My step dad was an alcoholic, and eventually, my mom became one, too; they were both drunks. There was a lot of foul language in our house, and a lot of verbal, physical, and emotional abuse. My half-sister, two half-brothers, and I were always scared and nervous, never knowing what would happen next.

Because I lived in such a volatile household, I didn't want to get married nor have kids. I did like having a boyfriend, though, and he convinced me that we should get married. I was a month past my seventeenth birthday, and Bob was just nineteen. The marriage lasted twenty-six years—surprisingly, because Bob was a terrible husband and terrible father to our four children.

Our marriage started out happily enough, but it wasn't long before Bob started smoking pot every day. For the last ten years of our marriage, I felt like a single mother because Bob refused to participate in anything concerning the kids. He seemed to have no interest in me, either, and he refused to go to counseling. It was when I realized that Bob was not interested in getting help that I decided to leave my marriage.

About a year later, when I was forty years old, I met the man who would become my second husband. I was having drinks with a girlfriend in a bar, and Carl approached me. Carl is black, and I am white, but our attraction to each other knew no color barrier. I was still legally married at the time, but that didn't seem to bother him. Carl told me that he was thirty, although I thought he looked younger. I later found out he was only twenty-six—just eight years older than my son—but by that time I was in love with him, and I didn't care how old he was.

We got married about five months after my divorce to Bob became final. At first, our marriage was good; if there was any sore spot, it was that he seemed to be a real momma's boy. Later on, however, I realized how small an issue that was, especially compared to his wanting to dress up. At first, it was just on Halloween—Carl would dress up as a woman, even putting on acrylic fingernails and he'd insist on going to his coworkers' Halloween parties. After the third Halloween party with Carl in drag, I asked him why he didn't choose a different costume.

"I like dressing up," he said simply.

Finally, I realized I'd been ignoring the signs. I put two and two together and approached my husband. "Carl, do you like to dress up in women's clothes? And not just on Halloween?"

He nodded. "Yes, sometimes."

After I learned his secret, it became routine on Friday and Saturday nights for him to dress as a woman. I would do his make-up, but of course, I couldn't do his make-up the way he wanted it done. We never went out on these nights; he cross-dressed to stay at home with me and watch TV. I once asked him, "Why do you get all dressed up if we're just going to sit here at home?" But he didn't answer me. Instead, he tucked his penis between his legs to make it look like he didn't have one.

After a night of watching TV dressed as a woman—or "Athena," as he called himself when he dressed up—he simply would go to bed. When he woke up the next day, he would be Carl again.

When I first met Carl, he was the most beautiful black man I'd ever seen. Well over six feet tall, he had a deep, resonant voice and imposing presence. Soon after we married, however, he began taking my hormone replacement medication and the herb black cohosh—he wanted to develop a bust. In the last years of our marriage, Carl actually had breasts. He went from being a totally flat chested man to a 36C bra size! We would go to Victoria Secret's and when I would buy a bra, he would buy a bra. He seemed pleased with his new body, but even worse, he showed little concern for how it affected me and our marriage. In fact I asked him if he was planning to cut his penis off because if so, then I was going to laminate it and place it on my keychain and call it the "Lorena Bobbitt" edition! This should have been a red flag, but I stayed with Carl because I had nowhere else to go. By this time, my children were grown and on their own, and I didn't want to impose on them. I think I'd known for years that my marriage was a sham, but I didn't want to accept it because it was easier to stay in the relationship than to try to fend for myself.

Then I began hearing that Carl was flirting with the women at work, and this really bothered me. Still, I stayed with him out of fear—I'd never lived on my own; I never lived by myself. I wasn't even sure who "I" was. Soon after I learned about Carl's flirting (and suspected he also was having affairs), he began to exhibit a violent temper. I have read statistical reports that suggest that some men with high testosterone levels who take hormone replacement medication can become quite moody. Usually, their temperament will balance out, but this wasn't the case with Carl. His temper was violent and erratic. I did the only thing I felt I could: I asked the pharmacist not to refill Carl's hormone replacement medication. Ultimately, I realized I needn't have bothered to speak to the pharmacist; Carl chose to stop taking the black cohosh and hormone replacement medication on his own.

This should have been another red flag, but I didn't see it until it was impossible to ignore it: The reason Carl stopped his medication was because he'd become involved with a new woman, and he didn't know how she would react to his having breasts.

My defining moment came when I realized that my husband was not cross-dressing for the woman with whom he was having an affair. After eleven years of living with Carl and supporting his cross-dressing, I was devastated to learn he'd become involved with someone for whom he was willing to give up his desire to look like a woman.

I finally decided to take the action; that I should had taken years ago, when I realized that Carl was obessing about who got what bra and who, heaven forbid would touch his lingerie; so I ended my marriage. You know that things are pretty sad when you have to ask your husband for nylons. Now, I'm living in a new state, with a new job … and I have a new life.

ROBERTA

~

When Roberta married her high school sweetheart, she thought she had everything she needed. But her new husband was already a broken man, traumatized by his experiences in Vietnam. Although she tried valiantly to help him cope, in the end her only recourse was to walk away. Today, fifty-five-year-old Roberta is a happily remarried social worker and lives in Key West, Florida.

I started dating Jimmy in high school, and I think what attracted me to him was that he always walked with a confident bounce in his step. He also was tall, blond, and good-looking.

He was drafted into the army at twenty-one and was sent to Vietnam. Just three months later he was severely injured in Cambodia when he was hit by a grenade. The entire right side of his body was essentially melted, including the right side of his face. After several weeks he was sent to a rehab center, and I finally was allowed to visit him. My heart was heavy as I walked though the door to his room; Jimmy was lying in his hospital bed, and it was true—half of his face had melted away, his fingers were webbed together, and he was blind in one eye. I sat at his bedside with tears streaming down my face. I closed my eyes because I couldn't accept what I was seeing. Listening to his voice with my eyes closed, I could believe he was still my same Jimmy. I held his hand and told him how much I loved him.

"Why love me when I look like this?" he asked.

But I loved him regardless of his appearance. I was so grateful he was still alive.

After a few months in rehab, Jimmy arrived home. As was common with Vietnam vets, however, he wasn't well received. He was shunned by strangers and friends alike. There were no parades, no yellow ribbons tied around trees. I was very angry and hurt by the way people treated Jimmy. But I was young and so I admit it was difficult for me to go out with him in public, knowing he'd be ridiculed for his disfigurements. I suppose I wasn't as supportive as I could have been. Still, I was deeply in love with him.

We got married in 1972, when I was twenty-two years old. We honeymooned in the Bahamas, which would have been idyllic, if not for our being there during a hurricane. On the third day of our honeymoon, the storm produced tremendous thunder and lightning. Jimmy became so nervous and anxious that I literally had to hold him by his underwear to prevent him from jumping off our seventh-floor balcony. I later learned that the thunder and lightning reminded him of the bombs dropping in Vietnam, but at the time, I had no idea what was going on with him. In those days there was no discussion about post-traumatic stress disorder (PTSD) and its ramifications.

Later that day, I found Jimmy hiding under the bed. When I asked what he was doing, he couldn't communicate with me. Jimmy was never able to talk to me about his Vietnam experience. I was so scared, and I didn't know how to help him. Still, I wasn't going to give up on the man I loved. Once we settled into our life as husband and wife, I did everything I could to keep him happy; I became a domestic goddess and tried to cater to him. But as much as I tried to provide love and care, he never was able to fully accept it. He seemed always to be testing me to see if I loved him.

About three years into our marriage, I surprised him with the news that I was pregnant. He was happy, even though he said he'd never wanted children. I, however, couldn't wait to have the baby, and I was thrilled when our daughter was born. Over the years we had two more children—sons—but Jimmy was not involved with any of them. He seemed unable to bond with them. Eventually, he started drinking heavily. I felt he was trying to drown his demons, even though he still was unable to speak with me about Vietnam. I continued to be supportive and kind, but I also was upset about his excessive drinking.

My concerns soon were validated in the worst way: One night while intoxicated, Jimmy drove his car head-on into another car, killing a passenger. Jimmy and the driver of the other car were severely injured.

I arrived at the hospital to find Jimmy lying on a gurney, bloodied from head to toe. His injuries were severe; in fact, I was told that his leg needed to be amputated. I begged the doctors not to amputate his leg. He'd never be able to handle it, I argued, not when he already had such physical disfigurement.

Distraught, I asked Jimmy if he could tell me how the accident happened. He replied dismissively that it was "just an accident." He showed absolutely no remorse. I was mortified.

Then we learned that, thankfully, the doctors had decided against amputation of his leg. I was proud of myself for arguing in Jimmy's behalf, but he simply shrugged, as if it were my job to take care of his needs.

That was my defining moment. I realized then that not only was Jimmy incapable of taking responsibility for his actions, but he also took it for granted that I would assume responsibility for him. Our relationship was always riddled with trauma, before getting married, and throughout the entire relationship there were very few peaceful times. It was pretty much one dramatic incident after the next. And that is the saga of an alcoholic home.

I know now that in lots of ways, Jimmy was a victim of circumstance. His war injuries and permanent disfigurement had a huge impact on the way that Jimmy viewed his life. He often felt that no one supported him—not his country, not his friends and family. I also think he tried to push me away because he did not feel he was worthy of the love that I tried so hard to give him.

I felt sad about the demise of our marriage. If only Jimmy could have accepted that he was at fault for the car accident; if only he would have appreciated all that I did for him. But he didn't. Ultimately, I simply couldn't help Jimmy anymore; I couldn't make him love me when he didn't love himself.

When I finally decided to end our marriage, it took me seven years and two lawyers to get a divorce. There was no great financial settlement—I got very little, monetarily—but I did get my freedom, and with that came a peace of mind I hadn't known in years.

About five years ago I met a wonderful man who eventually became my second husband. He is kind and patient, and we easily relate to each other. He is someone who does not push me away; rather, he has opened his arms wide to embrace my love.

BARBARA

~

Barbara was born and raised in Manchester, England, and came to the States as a teenager. She has three daughters, fathered by three different men, and says that her string of bad relationships has been due, in part, to her special gift—Barbara has visions. The visions, however, often frightened her so badly that she was afraid to live on her own. Because of this, she sought the companionship of men with whom she wasn't particularly well suited, just so she wouldn't be alone. Today, forty-nine-year-old Barbara, a Fragrance Specialist, no longer feels the need to become involved in relationships with men as a safety measure; she is well on her way to conquering her fears.

---

*A*s a child, I always admired my aunt Esther. She was my father's sister, and she and my uncle James had quite a loving relationship. Harsh words were never exchanged between them. In my mind, theirs was an idyllic marriage. My parents, however, were a different story. My father not only had affairs while he was married to my mother, but he also fathered other children, one of whom attended the same school as I. The situation was extremely embarrassing to me, and I think it somewhat tainted my opinion of men and relationships. My parents divorced when I was seven years old.

Like most little girls, I believed that when I grew up I would meet my Prince Charming; we would fall in love, and he would make me incredibly happy. It didn't work out quite that way for me, though, because I have never married. I have been in several long-term relationships, and I've even produced three daughters, but none of the men who fathered my children was anyone with whom I wanted to wake up with in the mornings for the rest of my life.

I had one of my longest relationships with Thomas, one of my co-workers with whom I carpooled. We eventually lived together for fifteen years, and he fathered one my daughters, but I see now that our relationship began for the wrong reason. I'd had a frightening experience one night and needed to see a friendly and familiar face, so I called Thomas to see if he would come over to stay with me. The experience might seem strange to most people, but it was commonplace for me; similar experiences occurred throughout my life.

I have always had vivid dreams that show me things that are about to happen—except that usually, I am not asleep while I'm "dreaming." I've correctly predicted the deaths of several close friends or significant people, and I also see people who are dead. Growing up, I was always frightened by these encounters because I knew that no one else could see these people. Although I came to understand my gift as I grew older, I was no less frightened by these occurrences; in fact, I became afraid of being by myself, particularly at night. I think that is one reason why I often stayed in relationships that were wrong for me—I just needed to have someone there with me.

I was thirty years old when my relationship with Thomas changed from him being my carpool mate to something more. One night, I had just put my daughters to bed and was preparing my work clothes for the next day. Suddenly, I heard a voice calling my name, and it scared me, because it was the same voice that I'd heard time and time again throughout my life. It particularly frightened me on this night, because I was living in a new house at the time, so my surroundings were relatively unfamiliar. It also scared me because it brought back memories of my childhood and how afraid I was then. Paralyzed by fear, I was unable to check on my daughters—I just took it for granted that they would be protected—but I was able to muster the courage to get out of the house. I remember running down the hallway, and stumbling down the stairs and out the front door.

I sat on the street curb, gripping it and holding on for dear life. I had my cell phone with me, and so I called Thomas. I told him simply that I was afraid to stay in my house by myself; he arrived within minutes.

It was always comforting to see a familiar face after I had one of my experiences, and seeing Thomas' face that evening was just the comfort that I needed. But in retrospect, I see that although Thomas got me through that particular night, I had no strategy for how I would continue beyond that point. I needed him that night, but he just never left.

He gradually moved in his belongings, a few at a time. I actually wasn't happy about it, but I felt there was nothing I could do—I was still so petrified to be by myself. "Things" were occurring in the house on a daily basis; it had reached a point that when I was sick and stayed home from work, I had to keep one of my children home from school to stay with me. I simply could not stay in that house by myself. I needed Thomas to stay there with me. He offered me protection.

Eventually, I began to think of us as a couple, which is what Thomas wanted, and I was grateful to him that I was finally able to sleep because he was there at night. It wasn't the best situation, though, and it probably wasn't helped by the fact that I became pregnant shortly after Thomas moved in. We also had financial issues; I made a significantly greater income than he did. I suppose some people may have thought he was using me to his financial advantage, but they didn't know that I was using him, too—for my own peace of mind.

After our daughter was born, I convinced Thomas to return to school. He did well and graduated with his bachelor's degree in business. I assumed he'd get a good job—he'd been working in my company's warehouse—but he didn't seem to have any ambition. Shortly after graduating from college, he was fired from his warehouse job. He did find another job more suited to his new status as a college grad, but he was fired from that one within a few months. After that he found a very promising pharmaceutical job with a prestigious company. Although that worked out for a few months, he eventually was fired because his employer felt that Thomas lacked drive and motivation.

I remained thankful to Thomas because I was able to sleep at night, but he and I were beginning to clash. Our relationship seemed extremely uneven to me. Thomas did help me to feel safe and secure, especially at night, but it seemed to me that I was doing all the work around the house. Thomas seemed incapable of helping with the housework or calling repairmen or fixing dinner; I did everything. And although he'd managed to find a menial job, I was making most of the money.

My defining moment came when I realized that my teenage daughter, who was working in a fast-food restaurant after school, was making more per hour than Thomas was making at his job.

And so I knew it was time to end our relationship, even though I was very torn. I'd had close to fifteen years of restful sleep at night, but Thomas was dragging me down with his own needs—it was more like having another child in the home than having an equal partner. I realized I was more afraid of being stuck in such an unbalanced and unfair relationship than I was of being alone. It was an ugly break-up; Thomas recognized how good he had it with me and didn't go quietly. But in the end, I got my freedom and was able to begin a new life.

Currently, my daughters and I live in a new home in the suburbs of Philadelphia. I've felt comfortable in this house since the day we moved in. It's the first place I've ever lived where I don't feel as though I need to have the lights turned on all the time. And I am most proud of the fact that I can now even sleep by myself without fear.

I still experience visions, but I have resigned myself to the fact that this is my gift, and I have been able to learn how to deal with it.

CASSIE

Thirty-six-year-old Cassie's beauty has often been compared to Halle Berry's. She is extremely sweet and somewhat naïve, which ultimately led her to bestow her trust in a man who continually betrayed her. Today, she's a financial advisor who lives in a small town in Rhode Island with her two children. She also continues to live with her husband for financial reasons.

---

*M*y mother felt stuck in an extremely painful marriage, and I suppose I grew up to unconsciously model her behavior. My father was extremely disrespectful toward my mother; during their marriage he had numerous affairs and produced at least a dozen children by other women. In addition to collecting woman, my father enjoyed collecting cars, boats, and airplanes. He took very good care of his worldly possessions, but was completely uncaring to my mother and to my brother and me. He was always very angry, very controlling, emotionally cold, and just plain mean.

My mother spent her married life trying to "keep the peace," because any little incident could set off my father into a rage—we were all terrified of him, yet my mother was more fearful of losing him. I could never understand what made her stay in such a situation, but she always justified her marriage by saying that my father was a "good provider."

I became pregnant when I was seventeen years old, and—perhaps surprisingly—both my parents stood by me. Steven, my daughter's father, soon left for college, and we eventually drifted apart. It was difficult to date anyone after that. Having a "ready-made family" was just too intimidating for most guys—except for Chuck.

Chuck had been a year behind me in high school, and I thought he was a geek. He was tall and lanky, wore thick glasses, and had a huge afro. I was not at all interested in him. When I ran into him a few years later, I almost didn't recognize him—he'd become quite an attractive young man. The angels in heaven must have been smiling on me because not only was Chuck very attractive, but he also still had a major crush on me. We began dating almost immediately.

My daughter was now three years old, and Chuck became like a father to her. He treated both of us very well and my daughter adored him. I was quickly falling in love with him. I got along very well with Chuck's family, too, even though I came to realize that Chuck's parents had something in common with mine—his father was a womanizer and very untrustworthy, and his mother stuck with him through it all. But I would soon find out there was a reason his mother stuck by his father's side—the two of them were swingers!

At that point in my life, I continued to be baffled by women like my mom and Chuck's mom, who stayed in relationships with men who cheated on them. Little did I know that once I married Chuck, my life would mimic theirs.

Chuck and I dated for about ten years, and during that time, Chuck proved that he was the total opposite of his father. He was very attentive to me, very considerate and caring. I was so in love with him, and I really wanted to marry him. When I would ask about marriage, though, Chuck would never give a definite answer. Finally, when I was twenty eight and Chuck was twenty seven, he proposed to me by hiding my engagement ring between the petals of a single red rose.

I'd spent a lot of time dreaming about getting married—I was dying to marry Chuck—but I think now that Chuck decided it was time to get married simply because it was the "right" thing to do after ten years of dating. I got caught up in the excitement of planning our wedding, but Chuck wasn't involved in any aspect of the planning phase. He just wasn't interested in helping. Even though I was very excited, a little voice inside me kept telling me that Chuck and I were not going to be together forever. I would quickly quiet that voice, figuring it must be pre-wedding jitters, and proceeded with the plans.

Chuck and I were married a year later, with two hundred fifty people in attendance. It was a beautiful, fairy tale wedding that took place in an actual castle in my hometown. I finally felt like the princess that I had always longed to be! It was all very romantic. Once we returned from our honeymoon, however, I remember thinking, "I'm married. Now what?"

About four months later, I noticed that Chuck was making a lot of cell phone calls to someone named Sheena. When I asked Chuck about it, he said she was a "friend." I think I knew it was not an innocent relationship, but I didn't want to admit it to myself—not even after I examined Chuck's cell phone bills and found out that he was calling Sheena more often than he called me.

Eventually, his "friendship" with Sheena ended, but my suspicions about Chuck began to increase. I eventually found out that he'd started calling someone new (I started checking the last number dialed on our phone), but when I confronted Chuck about this new woman, he insisted she was another "friend"; she was someone he was trying to help find a job. I knew he was lying; Chuck didn't have anything to do with the human resources department at his company, nor did he have any connections to anyone who could help find jobs. Still, I ignored the situation. I see now that I was modeling my mother, trying to "keep the peace." That little voice in my head, however, kept telling me that something was wrong.

When I was about seven months pregnant with our son, I received a phone call from a man who said he had information about my husband; that if I went to a particular motel I would find Chuck there. Chuck had said he was going over to a friend's house to watch a football game, but I knew I had to check out this information.

I immediately saw Chuck's car when I drove into the parking lot of the motel. I parked next to it and got out—and that's when I saw his wedding band in his car's cup holder. That could only mean one thing: He was in one of these motel rooms, and he was not alone. I went to the front desk, but was told that no one had registered under Chuck's name.

I went back to my car and waited. All I could do was sit in my car and wait for Chuck to come out of one of the rooms. After waiting for more than two hours, Chuck finally appeared. I got out of my car and approached him, asking what he was doing at the motel. He insisted he'd been watching the game in the motel's bar—a bar that I had already discovered was closed. He then tried to change his story, saying that he meant they were watching the game in one of the rooms; it was such an obvious lie.

Without another word to him, I got back in my car and drove home. I was seething and furious beyond words. It was the ultimate betrayal. Not only was Chuck cheating on me, but he was cheating while I was pregnant with his baby. I felt trapped; I was seven months pregnant and without any options.

When I gave birth to our son, I hoped that the excitement of having a new baby would spill over into our marriage and help get things back on track. That wasn't the case, of course; our relationship was never the same after I caught Chuck at the motel. Now, we hardly ever were intimate. His excuse was that he was too tired. He would come home from work and fall asleep in our living room, watching TV. We couldn't even have basic conversations with one another; Chuck always acted like something was wrong. I suspected that something was going on, especially because Chuck had become very secretive—when he took a shower, for instance, he would take his cell phone and car keys into the bathroom with him—but I didn't have any real proof that he was cheating on me.

I was just waiting for him to get sloppy with his routine. And then one day, he did just that—I discovered his car keys on our bed while he was showering. I quickly ran to his car and searched through it, hoping to find some sort of evidence. What I found left no doubt that Chuck was unfaithful. In a compartment in his car was a DVD from a camcorder. It was labeled "April 2004." With shaking hands, I took the DVD back into the house and then returned Chuck's keys to the bed where he'd left them. When he later left to go shopping, I played the DVD.

And that is when I had my defining moment. I knew conclusively that Chuck was not the one for me when I saw that he'd made a DVD of himself with another woman, in the act of cheating on me. It was a crushing blow to watch my husband have sex with someone else.

I felt physically ill as I called Chuck and told him to come home immediately. He seemed annoyed that he had to cut short his shopping trip, but maybe something in my voice told him that the balance of power had shifted. He came right home. I told him that I'd found the DVD in his car and that I'd *watched it*. I also told him that our marriage was over.

True to form, Chuck tried to tell me that he'd written the wrong date on the DVD and that it'd happened before we were engaged. Of course I knew that was a lie—if it had actually been that many years ago, he wouldn't even have known that DVD recorders existed. When Chuck realized that he literally had been caught in the act, he said over and over again that he was sorry and that he knew that he had messed up everything. His apologies meant nothing to me; he and I both realized that things between us could never be the same.

Following this incident, I spiraled into a deep depression. I couldn't sleep, couldn't focus, and I was consumed with thoughts that ate away at my self-esteem. Adding to the problem was the reality of the situation: Our marriage was over, but Chuck didn't move out of the house. And although I knew I should tell him that he had to go, I also knew that I could not afford the house by myself. I was completely torn up inside, and I didn't want my kids to think it was okay for a man to treat a woman the way Chuck treated me.

I decided to undergo therapy, where I learned that I'd been determining my own self-worth based on Chuck's actions. I'd convinced myself that something must be wrong with me and that was why Chuck had affairs. I'd forgotten that I was an attractive woman—intelligent, kind-hearted, and loving.

Chuck and I continue to live together, even though I want an end to this relationship. And I know that he is still seeing other women because I am constantly finding the evidence. Just the other day after he returned from a business trip in Amsterdam, Holland, he had an over the counter version of Viagra in his suitcase. I don't know why he would need that, except for the fact that he needed it for the other women, that he probably was having sex with while on his business trip. Yet, even knowing this, I recently allowed Chuck to move back into our bedroom. We've resumed being intimate with each other, but it's really as if we're just going through the motions. I guess that deep down I still love him and am hoping that he will change. I know this thinking is part of my self-destructive tendencies, but I can't help feeling as if I don't deserve better. I am basically repeating my parents' relationship. Still, I know that whenever I am financially able to do so, I will leave Chuck. I know this for sure.

LINDA

~

Linda is a thirty-two-year-old single mother of a fourteen-year-old son. Her most lasting relationship was fraught with deception and betrayal, yet she was so in love with the man that she often chose to ignore his affairs. Now, she has moved on and created a new life for herself and her son. She is a professional singer who is a contestant on a reality-based televised talent show and resides in Los Angeles.

My parents married when my mom was eighteen and my dad was nineteen years old. They had a beautiful relationship; when I think about it, it often brings me to tears. I envied the type of love they shared. My dad encouraged and supported my mom to be her own person. And as a result, he always did everything—from yard work to helping my mother clean the kitchen. Theirs is one of the most powerful relationships I've ever seen.

I have such fond memories of my childhood and my parents' relationship that I was somewhat unprepared for the realities of relationships. I'd always hoped to find a man who could emulate some of the positive, caring traits of my dad. I just assumed that I would find this perfect man, get married, have wonderful children, and—as sexist as it sounds—have a man to take care of me.

With all the nurturing and caring I received from my parents, it may be hard to believe that I found myself getting a home pregnancy test—I was a "good girl" who should have known better. I started seeing Frankie when I was seventeen. We dated briefly and had sex a few times—and then I got pregnant. I was terrified, mostly because I didn't know how my family would react. I needn't have worried on that score; my parents were terribly disappointed but they ultimately rallied around me. Meanwhile, Frankie and I were not getting along. We hadn't even been seriously dating—it was more like a fling. The boy I really cared about was Michael. He was my first love—the boy to whom I'd lost my virginity—but Michael was known for his wandering eye, and that always led to our breaking up. It was during one of our break-ups that I had the fling with Frankie. When Frankie found out that I was pregnant he was not at all supportive, so I essentially was left to raise our son by myself. (To this date Frankie has seen our fourteen-year-old son only three times.)

On a cold, snowy February night, three years after my son was born, I went to the supermarket—and bumped into Michael. He looked as handsome as ever, and we started chatting about how our lives were going. He was still in college and worked part-time. He'd been engaged, he said, but had broken it off. I tentatively told him about my situation—that I was living at home with my parents and my son, Jason. I had not really dated much since Jason's birth. My self-esteem was low, and I felt that no man would want to get involved with a struggling single mom.

Everything changed after that chance meeting in the supermarket. Michael and I started dating, and he understood that I had responsibilities to my son. Michael assured me his womanizing days were over. He promised to be faithful and to give Jason and me as much emotional support as he could. As the months went on, Michael and I spent all our free time together. Since he was an outdoors kind of man, we often went camping or picnicking, and we always included Jason in our excursions. My heart just melted when I saw the way that Jason bonded with Michael. I realized for the first time how important it was for Jason to have a father figure. And I felt more in love with Michael then, because he made my son feel special.

As excited as I was to be in love with Michael, my parents had their reservations about the relationship. They could never quite forget his history of womanizing, although they eventually grew to trust him and enjoyed being with him. His family, however, was another story. He had a very strong and domineering mother, whom he adored. His mother seemed to have such control over him, and he never spoke up for me—he felt caught in the middle.

It was clear that his mother didn't like me, but she never confronted me with her feelings; instead, she would complain to Michael about me. She didn't want me at their family functions. She expected that Michael would see his family on holidays, for example, and I would see mine—we would not go to any family functions together. It began to anger me that it seemed the only thing we did as a couple was sleep together.

After we'd been seeing each other for nearly six years—Jason was nine years old by this time—Michael and I finally decided to move out of our parents' homes and find a place together. My parents helped with the purchase of a farm (Michael was not doing well financially at this time), but to ease any wounded pride, I put Michael's name with my own on the deed.

By the time I was twenty-seven years old, I was overworked and had developed a heart condition called myocarditis. I was hospitalized for about a month, and my medical condition was very grave. When Michael visited me in the hospital, he would crawl into the bed with me and tell me all the wonderful things we were going to do, once I got healthy. One day after I returned home, Michael surprised me with a little green box from the jewelry store. He said "I'm really not supposed to show this to you yet, because the doctor said you shouldn't get excited." I suspected what the box held, though, so I was already trying to remain calm. Then Michael opened the box to reveal a beautiful ring, and Michael asked me to marry him. When we called our families with the news, my parents were excited for us, but Michael's mother said that she thought I got sick on purpose so that Michael would ask me to marry him. Her comments dimmed that shining experience for me, and she continued to put a damper on my excitement, especially when I found out that she had purchased my ring. Michael and I didn't plan a wedding right away, because it felt like we were walking on eggshells around his mother. We went one step at a time.

I regret that I didn't trust my instincts at that time in my life. I think I somehow knew that Michael would never make me a priority over his family, but I pushed that aside. I always felt if I kept the house clean and kept myself beautiful that I would be first in his life—but I never was. I was doing everything to please him, but inside, I felt something was wrong. When he gave me his paycheck so I could pay the bills, it was as though it was my reward for putting up with his family. Besides which, his paycheck barely covered our bills.

Then his brother-in-law offered him a position at his restaurant, which we thought would be the answer to our financial woes. What I never realized, however, was that this would come with a price tag—a staff filled with twenty-year-old waitresses. For Michael, working in that restaurant was like a crack addict living in a crack house. No matter how many lies he told to cover his activities, I knew that something was going on. Still, I didn't want to feel insecure; I just wanted to believe him. I wanted to believe that our life was good, clean, and strong. We had a beautiful house, and Michael had become a real father to Jason. I was madly in love with him, we had great sex, and he also was my best friend. I didn't want to believe that we were going in different directions, but it soon became apparent that we were.

The restaurant opened up a new opportunity for Michael; it gave him a chance to vent his frustrations to the girls who worked there. He confided in them about our relationship, his issues with his family, and our financial difficulties. Eventually, however, it became clear that he was doing more than just confiding in the girls. Suddenly, he began coming home at 3:00 AM., which he'd explain by saying that keeping late hours was just the nature of the restaurant business. I chose to ignore this obvious red flag.

By this time we'd been engaged for over a year, and I felt it was time to plan the wedding. Michael agreed, but it wasn't long before everything we planned was dissected by his family. I tried to involve his mother in my excitement, even to the point of calling her on the day I picked out my wedding gown. But her response to my announcement was to say, "I don't think my son wants to marry you." Michael, she informed me, could manage much easier financially on his own.

Michael never admitted that he was involved in affairs, but I suspected that he was, and that he probably was involved with more than one of them. Eventually, he had to unburden himself, and he confessed that he had been unfaithful.

I was completely devastated by his confession, and so I called off the wedding—just two months before we were to get married. Our invitations were already printed, the wedding hall was booked—and now it was all for nothing. He didn't want to move out, but I couldn't live with his betrayal, nor was I willing to be a maid in his hotel. So we separated.

Then September 11th happened, and that really affected us emotionally. I would watch TV every day and see the people searching for their fiancées or spouses. Their loss was so acute, and there was no way to ease their pain. Michael and I decided to get back together. It was very hard for me, because I didn't trust him anymore. Still, I let him move back in with Jason and me and in February, we began to plan for a small wedding. I think he agreed to it just to please me, because as our wedding day got closer, I realized that he hadn't told his family we were getting married. This was quite upsetting to me, but it was even more upsetting when he asked me to tell his family for him.

I agreed to talk to his mother, even though this was the last thing I wanted to do. The next morning I called her and asked if I could come over the next day. *My defining moment occurred at this meeting with his mother. I showed up with bagels and coffee and his mother proceded to ask me what was I planning to wear to the wedding (one of Michael's cousins was getting married in the coming weeks) and I told her that I was planning to where a white dress with little diamonds on it. She looked at me in aghast and mentioned that it was inappropriate for me to wear white to her nephew's wedding. It was then that I realized we were talking about two different weddings, I of course was talking about my own wedding and I informed her of such. Instead of graciously offering her congratulations and best wishes, she chose to inform me that Michael was having an affair with an eighteen-year-old waitress at the restaurant and had no intentions of marrying me.*

His mother looked at me, smiling triumphantly, while my heart felt broken and betrayed. Michael could have told me about the affair himself—which would have been bad enough—but instead, he sent me to see his mother. He must have known that she couldn't wait to tell me about his affair

Shortly after his mother's pronouncement, Michael walked into the house with a broad smile on his face and asked brightly, "How are my favorite girls?"

I glared at him. "Your mother has just explained to me that you're involved with a waitress," I answered, "and that you do not want to marry me."

I think he realized it was pointless to try to deny it. I told him once again that we were finished and that he had to move out. He quickly moved back home with his mother.

Jason was as sad as I was that my relationship with Michael had ended. But I was even more devastated when I learned a few weeks later that Michael and the eighteen-year-old were getting married within the month. It was heart-wrenching for me to think of him marrying someone else.

Within a week after his wedding, Michael called me, saying he wanted to see me on the side. Maybe I was trying to get back at his teenage bride, because I actually agreed, and we got together a few times. Then I finally realized that it was time for me to grow up and get back my self-respect. I told Michael that we were over and that he should not call me again.

I never heard from him after that day, but at times I still look at the phone in hopes that he will call. I'm having a difficult time getting him out of my system.

Currently, I'm taking one step at a time and trying to focus on my son. Although I admit I've wanted to call Michael, I remind myself of my "defining moment," and I resist the temptation to call him. I tell myself that he is unworthy of me and that I am so much better than he allowed me to realize. So far, repeating that mantra has worked for me.

ELLEN

〜

Liberal-minded Ellen successfully "dodged a bullet" by ending her relationship with ultra-conservative John *before* agreeing to marry him. She admits she ignored some serious red flags while they were dating, but her strong will and good sense ultimately prevailed. Now forty-one years old and in a more equitable and loving relationship, Ellen, who is a model and her significant other currently reside with their two-year-old daughter in Orange County, California.

I grew up as the youngest of six children and was raised by my mom and stepfather. They had a loving relationship, and I always hoped to find such happiness when I got married. I envisioned finding my Prince Charming, who would be supportive of me and my career. We would work together to achieve the things we needed and desired.

Unfortunately, life isn't a fairy tale. Ted, my first husband, was very strange—actually, I think he might have had some type of mental disorder. He seemed very passive-aggressive and by the end of our relationship, he became psychotic. When we finally divorced, I decided that I would wait before getting involved with a man again.

I changed my mind about waiting, though, when I reconnected with an old friend. John and I knew each other in high school—at the time, he was my best friend's boyfriend. I lost contact with him after he and Sharon broke up, but thirty years later, Sharon happened to run into John again, which led to our reconnecting, too. I learned that John was now divorced and had a fifteen-year-old daughter.

We started dating and had a lot of fun together. I enjoyed talking to him, especially about history, a topic we both enjoyed. The only issue that surfaced in our otherwise great relationship was religion. John considered himself a Christian, while I am a pagan. Although I mentioned my beliefs on our first date, John made a joke of it, telling me that there was "a motorcycle gang known as the Pagans." As we continued dating, he sometimes would make comments about how he knew he was going to heaven, and he could only hope that I would make it there, too. Eventually, I came to realize that although John was Christian, he had a lot of prejudices. He was against blacks, gays, and anyone else who was not like him.

I always wondered how he could call himself a Christian whenever it was convenient for him. He would also still question whether I was getting into heaven since I'm a pagan. But I always told him that my God was as big as the universe and he's letting everyone into heaven—even the Christians!

John also revealed his need to be in charge. Now, my mom had raised us girls to believe that we could be anything we wanted to be. She instilled in us the importance of being able to take care of ourselves, without relying on a man. At the very least, I wanted a relationship that was an equal partnership, and it was beginning to seem as if that wouldn't be the case with John. He wanted me to be a part of *his* dream; he wanted me to leave my job, sell my house, and relocate with him out of state—and this was only six months into our relationship. When I tried to explain my need for independence and equality to John, he'd insist that he was just showing me how much he cared. I didn't know what to do, and unfortunately, I did not follow my instincts. Instead, I allowed myself to fall in love with him.

Soon, John started pressuring me to get married. I had only been divorced a few years, and I wasn't sure that I ever wanted to be married again. But the more I seemed hesitant, the more John tried to rush our relationship. I remained uneasy, though, because he also was becoming more and more domineering.

My defining moment, when I realized that John was not the one, occurred after we'd had a small disagreement, and John informed me that when a woman and man cannot agree on any issue, then the man has to dominate. The man is always right, he insisted, because the Bible said so!

When he told me this, it really did finish our relationship for me. I finally came to the obvious conclusion that socially, politically, and religiously, he was a complete contradiction of my being very liberal. I'd also grown tired of his constantly trying to impose his beliefs on me.

I ended our relationship and also regained my self-respect. I asked myself how could I have possibly been involved with a man who treated me as a second-class citizen and who never valued my opinions. I guess I just enjoyed his attention, and I was momentarily blinded by it.

I don't see myself ever marrying again—there are too many legal ramifications, such as community property and joint taxes. Still, that doesn't mean I won't be involved with someone.

About nine months after my breakup with John, I met Ryan. He's fifteen years my junior—he's twenty-six and I'm forty-one—and maybe that would be a red flag for some people, but Ryan is the love of my life. He's extremely sensitive and supportive, and he encourages me in my pursuits. I think it's kind of a generational thing, because he was born in the post-women's lib, feminism, and equal rights era. As a result, he never thought of women as anything but equal to men. His parents had a very good relationship, and they encouraged each other's dreams, differences, and goals.

I call my relationship with Ryan a "partnership," because we're not married, but I don't consider him a boyfriend (that seems too adolescent). We now have a little girl whom we co-parent.

Initially, my parents were shocked by our age difference, but now they respect Ryan's values and his strong work ethic. They realize that I've found the right man for me. And together, Ryan and I are raising our daughter to think for herself, be independent, and never let anyone stifle her or hold her back. It's a lesson I've finally learned for myself.

CHRISTINA

～

Christina owns a construction company in Salt Lake City, Utah—a far cry from the life she earlier envisioned for herself. The only child of a wealthy couple, Christina had a privileged upbringing. She expected to marry a man who would provide her with a lifestyle much like that of her parents, and her relationship with a corporate mogul seemed set to ensure that she would have that opulent and extravagant lifestyle. But Christina eventually realized that everything comes with a price, including the life she'd envisioned. In the end, she was unwilling to pay it.

Today, Christina enjoys a simple life filled with simple pleasures. Her greatest joy is spending time with her husband—the man she met after leaving the corporate mogul—and their five children.

I was twenty-eight years old when I met Alan, and I should have left him at "hello." But many women who are not married at twenty-eight reach a panic point, and I suppose I was one of them. I'd begun to wonder if I ever would get married.

My parents were in more of a panic than I was. They wanted to see me settle down and be as happy as they have been. At the time, they were approaching their fiftieth wedding anniversary—definitely a good example of how a marriage should work. My parents, however, didn't seem to understand modern-day relationships. After they met and started dating, they were married within five months. They still can't grasp that their situation was not the norm.

I was once engaged to an airline pilot, and my parents were thrilled, but they did not like the fact that we wanted to be engaged for two years before the wedding. Eventually, we decided to call off the wedding, which made our long engagement seem fortuitous—better a broken engagement than a messy divorce—but my parents still kept hoping I'll meet and marry someone without waiting so long.

Since breaking off my engagement, I've dated a succession of men—it seems everyone wants to set me up with someone. Some guys seemed worth keeping, but when my father would ask them where our relationship was headed, they would head for the door.

I suppose my standards were rather high. I expected that my husband would have a career with a corporate position and that he'd provide a good income. I anticipated that I would become a stay-at-home mom, while also attending fancy events with my husband or accompanying him when he traveled for business. I wanted the big house with a maid and all the good stuff. But, of course, reality turned out to be a little different.

Alan and I met while I was studying for my CPA. He lived in a different town at the time, which I liked, because I felt I'd be less distracted—he lived too far away for us to go out every weekend. Alan seemed perfect. He was very mature for his age and was articulate, friendly, well-mannered, and considerate. He had a good job as assistant manager in a corporate accounting firm and could afford to provide me with the lifestyle that I had come to expect. For our first date, we went out to dinner at a beautiful restaurant. We talked for several hours and determined that since we both wanted and expected the same types of things in life, we would make a good couple. And so our relationship began.

And it was a very "safe" relationship. Because Alan could not spend every weekend with me, there wasn't that constant pressure to go out every Friday night, just because that was what couples do. But when we were together, Alan was extremely thoughtful. He would always take me to such beautiful places, and when I visited him in his town, he would bend over backwards to show me around or to meet his friends. When we were apart, he would send me roses. I really thought we were heading down the marriage road.

Of course, Alan wasn't exactly perfect; I realized that he did have some quirks. One big "quirk" was that for five months, we were not sexually involved. He was very romantic, and we would kiss, but he never suggested becoming intimate. He wanted our relationship to be based on friendship first, he'd tell me, which made perfect sense to me. When we finally made love, it seemed to be okay for us—not great fireworks, but we certainly were compatible. Then, within the next few weeks, my relationship with Alan began to change. He was on a business trip and had sent me a ticket to join him. He suggested we could go shopping together. Because we now had an intimate relationship, I assumed that we'd progressed past the "friends" stage and that we might be shopping for an engagement ring. Instead, we spent hours in some exclusive men shops while Alan carefully picked out underwear and socks.

Serious red flags began to wave for me during that shopping excursion. I thought Alan's attention to detail in choosing underwear was slightly bizarre, especially as we then had no time to do anything else, but when we returned to his corporate apartment, I discovered something truly bizarre—his bedroom drawers contained literally hundreds of neatly folded underwear and socks. I realized that Alan was a bit obsessive-compulsive.

Several weeks later, I was to meet Alan for lunch with his co-workers. When he arrived to pick me up, he had a sweater for me—not as a gift but because he felt I needed to change into "something a little nicer." I was offended, because I felt I already was dressed quite nicely, afterall, I was wearing a sweater which was purchased at Nordstrom. Alan was beginning to seem overly concerned with appearances, and in the process, he would criticize me.

After that, it became very clear that Alan was trying to change me in other ways. He told me that if I wanted to proceed in our relationship (a clear reference to marriage) that I would have to change my taste in music. And that was just the beginning; he commented on several other things that I would have to "change" in order to maintain a relationship with him. Obviously, he wanted a relationship only on his own terms.

My defining moment came when I visited Alan for what would be the final time. He'd taken me to his office on a Saturday because he had to pick up some work, but he wouldn't let me follow him into the office unless I promised to keep my coat on—he didn't want anyone who might be there to see my clothes.

Now I know that I was wearing extremely nice clothing and I was completely offended and appalled. There were only two other people in the office in the first place—a janitor and a frumpy secretary working on a report at the front desk. Besides, there was absolutely nothing wrong with what I was wearing. Alan just seemed to enjoy trying to make me feel inadequate.

Let's just say, it was not a pleasant visit. On the last day of my visit, I purposely wore a pair of jeans and my oldest sweater and my tennis shoes. *As I said good-bye to Alan for the last time in my life, and informed him that there was no longer a need for him to call me because the relationship was over—it brought me total satisfaction to do so, as I stood in front of him dressed from head to toe in items I purchased from Target!*

I'm the first to admit that I like nice things, and Alan could have provided them for me. But I know I made the right decision; my self-respect has no price tag.

Now, I am married to a wonderful, down-to-earth, fun-loving man. He's not someone I would have envisioned myself with when I was younger—he works with his hands, not corporate accounts—but I couldn't be happier. We've been married for fourteen years, and in addition to his being a wonderfully warm, considerate husband, he's also a wonderful father to our children. I am living blissfully with the true love of my life.

ANDREA

～

Andrea is a forty-two-year-old career-minded woman. She waited until she was in her thirties before she married, thinking that would be a better guarantee of success. But Andrea soon learned that even mature, established, and wise women can makes mistakes in judgment.

Fortunately, the abuse she suffered at the hands of her husband is now history, and Andrea has emerged as a stronger and more self-assured woman. Today, she is a successful sales associate for a well-known architecture magazine and enjoys life in Boston with her three daughters.

I guess I used to be somewhat delusional. I actually thought that when I married, my life would be perfect. I thought that my husband would be an amazing man and that he would be mature, rich and madly in love with me.

Instead, I married a man who, as I later found out, despises women.

I was thirty-two years old when I met Terrence. He was thirty-eight. I had two daughters from previous relationships, and Terrence had two children from his first marriage. I was impressed by the way he communicated—his words were rich and fluid—and we spent hours talking on the telephone. He was very smart and extremely well-read.

It seemed that we had a lot in common—we loved the same kind of music, and we both enjoyed reading and participating in various discussion groups. We got along fantastically.

In fact, we got along so well that on the day that marked the first anniversary of our first date, Terrence and I eloped.

My family wasn't pleased by our elopement. My mother had wanted me to have a big wedding, but my father wasn't annoyed because we eloped; he was annoyed because he didn't particularly care for Terrence. He knew that I was making more money than Terrence, and my dad held the old-fashioned belief that the man should be the bread winner in the relationship. Because Terrence worked as a probation officer, his profession just didn't "cut it" in my father's mind.

But I didn't care; I wasn't assessing what Terrence could or could not do for me financially. I just knew that I loved him. In retrospect, however, I see that I didn't evaluate my relationship with Terrence as objectively as I should have. Having just gotten out of a previous relationship, all I cared about at the time was that Terrence was completely unlike my former boyfriend. I spent so much time comparing Terrence to the previous boyfriend that I had a difficult time seeing Terrence for who he was. I see now that I ignored the red flags.

One red flag should have been that many of my friends didn't like Terrence; they thought he was volatile and crazy. I didn't see it that way, of course; I just described him as "aggressive," a trait that can be positive in some situations. I suppose that little voice inside of me did tell me not to get involved with Terrence, but I kept choosing to ignore it.

I soon found out that I should have listened. Three months after we had eloped, I had my first indication that something was not quite right with Terrence. We had a heated argument over my decision to keep my maiden name—to him, that was a major insult, and he was very angry. Later that same day, Terrence got into an argument with one of his female coworkers over something trivial. But Terrence had gotten so angry that he took his metal hole-puncher and hit this coworker several times on her head! She needed medical treatment. Terrence was terminated from his job immediately and was made to attend anger-management courses.

Shortly after that incident at his office, Terrence became abusive toward me.

The abuse began very slowly and very subtlety. I noticed that he was becoming very easily irritated, demanding, and somewhat controlling. He would intimidate me by standing really close to me as he shouted at me, and then he would break objects around the house. After the birth of our daughter, his anger escalated to the point that he began hitting me.

The first time he hit me, I was so ashamed that I couldn't tell anyone. I wasn't the stereotypical woman who was associated with domestic abuse; I was an educated, successful, mature career woman. I was scared, but I also felt stupid and hoodwinked. My girlfriends had seen the potential in Terrence to become violent, but I had ignored the signs.

The first time he hit me, I logically realized that this would be the first of many times if I didn't end our marriage, because I was smart enough to know that once abuse begins, it never stops. But I stayed with Terrence, because I knew that I had to develop a strategy to get out of the relationship safely and so I could protect my family. The longer I stayed with Terrence, however, the more I discovered that he had deceived me prior to our marriage. He had presented a side of himself that he wanted me to see so that I would be attracted to him; in reality, he was quite a different man.

Then, Terrence began isolating me from my friends and family. He wanted to monopolize all of my time. We quickly fell into a pattern of only participating in activities of his choosing.

I was just beginning to think that maybe the physical abuse was a one-time thing—Terrence was often angry, but he hadn't raised his hand to me again. But when I was pregnant with our daughter, his verbal abuse and anger seemed to escalate. And after the birth, the physical abuse began. He would punch me and kick me and throw me down on the ground; then he would kick me some more. By this time, most of our arguments revolved around the fact that our sex life had become nonexistent and, of course, that angered him. Even though I never verbalized my hatred for him, he knew, because I couldn't hide it from him. My actions spoke volumes. I believed that this made things even worse between us, because he felt rejected. But I wasn't interested in him sexually anymore. In fact, I wasn't even interested in him as a human being anymore.

Sometimes, I'd just keep peace in the house, I would have sex with him, but I would hate those nights because it felt like rape. I thought I was protecting my daughters and my parents from being harmed by him, so I couldn't tell Terrence that I was completely disinterested in him. He couldn't understand that after he was abusive to me, there was nothing about him that I loved. And if there was nothing about him to love, there was certainly nothing that would make me feel as though I wanted to make love to him.

I believed our relationship was being played out quite differently in Terrence's own mind. He felt that he was madly in love with me and was trying to make things work between us (if he hit me, he would always apologize). He couldn't understand why I seemed indifferent toward him.

My defining moment occurred one night after Terrence beat me in front of my two daughters. I remember thinking that my daughters must never witness anything so horrific happening to their mother ever again.

They had heard the screaming and fighting between us on several occasions, but they had never seen Terrence actually strike me. That night, however, they watched as Terrence punched me and slapped me and threw me across a room, and I knew that those images would be indelibly imprinted in their minds. I had been trying to protect them from Terrence's rage by taking all his abuse myself, but now I realized that in doing so, it seemed as if his behavior should be tolerated. I knew then that my daughters and I had to leave that night.

We ran to a neighbor's house, and Terrence didn't try to follow us. It was just as simple as that. For months I had tried to formulate a strategy to leave him, but on that evening, we simply … left. Just like that.

In spite of everything, my daughters and I are pretty well-adjusted. I never pressed charges against Terrence—I was relieved just to get away from him, and I didn't want to face court proceedings. Life has a way of balancing itself, though—I recently learned that Terrence was sentenced to three years in prison for assault after he beat up a coworker.

My marriage to Terrence definitely empowered me because it gave me a stronger sense of my own ability to accomplish things. As soon as I was free of him, my career took off. I have advanced several times in the corporation where I work, and I am proud of the fact that I will be able financially to send all three of my daughters to college.

Today, I look at men with a discerning eye. I am more careful about the men I choose to date, and I also recognize my own shortcomings, which has helped me to improve myself immeasurably.

DEBRA

~

Debra expected her life to mimic her parents' idyllic existence, and when she met Kyle, she was sure she was on her way. Although she was married for twenty-two years, she suffered in silence for most of that time, as her husband had several affairs and essentially disregarded and disrespected his family. Now forty-five and divorced, Debra has turned her life around. She works as a licensed practical nurse in Atlanta, Georgia, and is blissfully single.

---

*M*y parents have been married for sixty years. They had an old-fashioned marriage when I was growing up—my mom stayed at home and my dad worked. They clearly love each other very much, and because of their excellent modeling, I always thought that love would last forever. Also based on my parents' marriage, I assumed the man I married would help with running the household, help with the kids. My dad was the breadwinner, but he always was very involved with my siblings and me. So when it came time for me to be in a relationship, I was expecting it to be a fifty/fifty arrangement. I was wrong.

Kyle and I met in high school and married when I was nineteen and Kyle was twenty. Unlike my loving parents, Kyle's parents divorced when he was thirteen. His dad had a drinking problem, and he abused Kyle's mom for years. He also had a steady girlfriend throughout his marriage to Kyle's mom.

My family did not like Kyle. This was partly due to the fact that Kyle didn't go to college, and they felt I needed someone with a college education. Kyle was working as a refrigeration technician when we got married, but he went through a number of jobs because he was extremely lazy.

There were red flags in our relationship, even before we married, but I was only a teenager and so I didn't see any of them. I knew about Kyle's family history, but I thought our relationship was going to be different because he seemed to really care for me and was really romantic. After four or five years of marriage, though, the romance faded. I thought that if we had kids, things would be better for us.

Kyle began an affair with Jen, one of his coworkers, while I was pregnant with our first child. During this time, Kyle left me, saying he would never come back because he no longer loved me. But after our son was born, he moved back home. Although my family disliked him even more when they found out about his affair, they wanted my marriage to work because we have no divorce in my family.

One day while I was shopping with a friend, we happened to see Jen and her baby. My friend casually asked me if I knew that Jen's husband had testicular cancer. She mentioned it as a way to tell me that Jen's baby couldn't have been fathered by her husband; he was unable to reproduce because of his cancer. The shock of this news caused me to literally pass out. It was obvious that Kyle was the father of Jen's baby. In fact our oldest daughter, was born just three months before my husband's love-child. As a matter of fact our daughters are in the same Girl Scout troop and are not even aware that they are sisters.

I was devastated, yet I continued to try to salvage my marriage. I knew Kyle was still having affairs—this continued for several years. He even reached a point of telling me that he was seeing someone, that he was having sex with his latest girlfriend while I was home taking care of our kids—we had three children by this time. During this time my appearance changed. I gained a lot of weight, and I let myself go. I suppose I ate to console myself.

As time went on, I realized that even though I still loved Kyle, I couldn't live with him, knowing he was seeing other women. Just about this time, however, Kyle came to his own decision. He promised me that he was finished cheating on me and that he would never do it again. He said we needed to grow old together.

My defining moment—when I realized that Kyle was not the "one"—came, oddly enough, long after his affairs had ended. It had nothing to do with other women; instead, it was because of Kyle's complete selfishness and disregard for his family.

Kyle developed a fascination with snakes, and he decided that he would begin breeding them.. It made no difference to him that I was petrified of snakes or that having snakes around our small children might not be the best idea. When I learned that he took $5,000 from our savings account—our emergency money—to buy snakes and equipment to breed them, that really was the beginning of the end for me. Some of these snakes grew to be twenty feet long. In fact he decided to move one of them into our bedroom—that's when I deceided to move into one of our spare rooms. Initally, he had all of these snakes (and rats and mice for feeding) in our attached garage but for some reason he insisted on bringing that one particular twenty foot snake into the bedroom. One day I came home with the kids and as we walked through the front door, we could hear Kyle screaming from the bedroom. Evidently he had just finished playing with the feeding mice and rats (something you should not do before playing with a python) and one of the pythons had his whole arm in its mouth and the tips of Kyle's fingers were already gone. We were told by the paramedics that had we reached home a half hour later, he would have been dead. And for a second, I regretted that fact that I did not take an extended trip to the park with the kids before arriving home.

Immediately after this incident, I told Kyle to gather up his reptiles and equipment; our marriage—and my suffering—was over.

We now have been divorced for several years, and I thank God every day that I was strong enough to end my marriage to Kyle. I've moved on, and I now live a quiet, stress-free (and snake-free) life with my kids—and my sanity.

NICOLE

~

Nicole thought she'd found the man of her dreams. Well-educated, articulate, and charming, he seemed to be everything she wanted in a husband. Yet even when he began to exhibit less impressive qualities, Nicole's strong sense of honor and commitment caused her to feel trapped by her promise to marry him.

Now a hospital administrator, forty-four-year-old Nicole happily resides with her second husband and their three-year-old son in a suburban community near Chicago.

My parents had a very unhappy marriage, partly because of the hours that my father worked—he was either asleep during the day or at work at night. He was not a participant in my family's day-to-day life. My parents divorced when I was six years old, so my mother and maternal grandmother raised me, and they always instilled in me the need to be a self-sufficient African American woman who is ever mindful of the financial aspect of a relationship. My grandmother always collected my grandfather's paycheck from him and immediately deposited the funds into her personal account.

It may have been because I watched my parents' marriage break up, but I developed a firm belief that if I started something, I would see it through to the end, regardless of what the outcome may be. As a result of this belief, I think I often ignored the red flags in my relationships.

William was really my first boyfriend. We met when I was twenty-six and he was thirty-two. I thought he looked clean-cut and really handsome, and I was immediately attracted to him.

William was a professional photographer, so he had an eye for beauty and he loved art of all kind. In fact, William introduced me to art—we spent hours at the Chicago Art Museum—and he helped me develop an appreciation for it. William also could build or fix almost anything. I was impressed by the amount of patience he displayed while building or fixing things. His precision and his creativity were a major turn-on to me.

William educated me on art, while I educated him on religion, sharing my love of the Bible with him. I have strong Christian values, and I was able to evoke William's spiritual side. This was all new to William. We regularly attended church together, and I loved him for that.

But even though I was already in love with William's qualities, and I loved that he introduced me to art and culture, I couldn't accept the fact that as a freelance photographer, William did not have a full time job. He also did not have a college degree—an important point, as in my family, we highly value education.

My mom was concerned about my relationship with William; she did not particularly care for him, although she was always cordial to him. William's mother, however, loved me as though I were her own daughter, and I loved her in return.

After we'd been dating about a year, I accepted a one-year fellowship position in Dubuque. The only problem was that it was three hours away from Chicago, where William lived. Although we could visit each other on weekends, William was not happy that I accepted the fellowship, and we had several heated arguments. Just before I was due to leave, however, he surprised me with a ring and a proposal of marriage, and I accepted. It was hard to leave William after that, but I was off to start my fellowship, leaving William to make our wedding plans.

I began making friends with others in the fellowship program, and that is how I met Clifford. He wasn't tall or handsome like William, but he did have a PhD in philosophy. And just like William, he loved art; we would often go to the local art galleries or museums or go out for coffee together. It was a strictly platonic relationship; Clifford was a total gentleman. I really enjoyed our conversations. I could talk to him about anything, and he always seemed interested. I continued to visit William on the weekends, but often, I spent my time alone at his apartment, because he was photographing a wedding or a show. During these visits, as I sat by myself, I found myself thinking about Clifford. Eventually, I started spending time with *Clifford* in Chicago while William was working. Our relationship was still platonic, but one night over coffee, Clifford confessed that he was interested in me romantically, and he wanted me to call off the wedding to William. I realized that night that I was very emotionally involved with Clifford. I left feeling overwhelmed and confused. I really did want to follow through on marrying William (because I always keep my word), but I decided that I needed to call off the wedding. William was understandably distraught and angry, but he just calmly informed me that he planned to continue to pursue me. Then I told Clifford that I'd broken up with William, but I needed some time to myself so I could think clearly. I put all of my focus into work.

William continued to try to persuade me to marry him; he was so persistent that it was extremely hard not to give in. He always had been in control and was so charismatic that at the end of my fellowship, I began to see things his way. Once again, I accepted his marriage proposal. Now, William feverishly began making plans for a big wedding. Not a detail was spared. He handled everything; the only thing I did was choose my dress. And I buried the fact that I was marrying William not out of love but out of my obligation to keep my word.

So, with over two hundred guests in attendance, William and I were married. We went on a six-night cruise for our honeymoon, and then returned to the condo that William had found as our new home (without any input from me). We could have easily lived close to both of our families and to our jobs in Chicago, but William intentionally chose a place that was nearly an hour away from Chicago—he didn't want my mother just dropping in on us. We were so far away from my family that my mother would often check the train schedule to determine which train I would be on and she would go to the station and stand on the platform in hopes of seeing me ride passed her.

Soon, William's obsessive need for control became even more obvious. I began to notice that he was keeping track of the amount of panty-liners I was using in a given day. And he would constanly ask me what was happening to them and why did I feel the need to change my panty-liners twice a day. He started keeping a log of where I was at any given minute of the day, and he noted how many times a day I took a shower or what time I came home from work.

But my *defining moment came, eighteen months into my marriage, once he decided to initiate a letter writing campaign against me. My girlfriends and family members called to inform me that they had received a disturbing letter from William, in fact I later discovered that William had sent out this disturbing letter to all 200 guests that attended our wedding. The letter was bizarre and did not make too much sense, but the contents of the letter that the readers could decipher were extremely embrassing. He mentioned that I shaved my pubic hairs and put powder down there. He also included copies of the cards that Clifford sent me while I was doing my fellow-ship. He even sent a letter to my mom telling her that I would be severing all communication with her.*

I was absolutely livid and could not believe that he would do something so unkind and controlling. When I confronted him about it, he simply stared at me, and this lack of response was even more maddening.

Enough was enough. It was at that point that I told William that I was leaving him. I packed my things and left for my grandmother's house that evening. While I was staying there, William would come over every day, begging me to return. He also began following me everywhere—to my job, when I went out to eat, when I visited with friends. He seemed to always be watching me. Finally, I filed a restraining order, and William later was arrested for stalking me, and he spent some time in jail. My decision to divorce him was an easy commitment to keep. I have learned, however, that I do not need to follow through with everything, especially when that follow-through causes pain. I have learned that sometimes, promises simply need to be broken.

MONICA

~

Monica is a planner—she understands the value of effective organization. If anyone had told her she'd fall for Steve, an inveterate free spirit, she would have laughed. But sometimes opposites do attract—at least initially.

Although even Monica couldn't have planned for the turn her life has taken, she feels more confident and self-assured today than she was during her seven-year marriage. Now separated for nearly a year, forty-four-year-old Monica and her three-year-old daughter live together in Cheyenne, Wyoming, where Monica earns her living as an artist.

---

*M*y dad was brilliant, but although he had a degree from an Ivy League college, he never achieved his professional goals. Still, my parents were both concerned with outside appearances, and so they stayed together and played the part of a professional couple because it "looked" better.

Growing up in tiny Sheridan, Montana, I felt isolated and alone. I had crossed eyes and a hip deformation, and my mom felt I was chubby. I was constantly teased at my school because of my appearance. I was sent away to boarding school when I was fifteen and my parents were in the process of getting divorced. Later, I worked my way through college, taking eight years to do it because I never asked my parents for support.

I didn't date much in college. Although I'd transformed myself physically, I guess I still felt like the Ugly Duckling, even though my friends told me I'd become a swan. I met Steve when I was thirty-five and he was twenty-nine, and he was the first man with whom I ever had a warm and ongoing relationship.

Steve was incredibly spontaneous—he never planned anything; he always wanted to just "go with the flow." I, on the other hand, was always well organized, and so his lack of planning bothered me. Still, he seemed so much better than any guy I had gone out with up to that point, so I was unable to see his complete spontaneity as a problem.

We became engaged within five months of meeting each other, and married soon after that. After honeymooning in Hawaii, we returned home to settle into married life. We bought a house, but Steve was nervous about handling the responsibility; his method of coping with this nervousness was to do nothing around the house. We had some other issues over the next few years, including my losing my job and becoming ill. Eventually, though, Steve and I got back on track financially, and my health improved to the point where we decided to try to have a baby.

Unfortunately, I had fertility issues—it was very difficult for me to conceive. To make matters worse, my in-laws tried to step in and take over by ordering fertility medication for me. I took it in spite of their interference—I was desperate to conceive—but then they called every month to ask if I was pregnant yet. Finally, I did become pregnant, and when our daughter was born, Steve and I both were ecstatic. Our life seemed perfect.

Unfortunately, our "perfect" life quickly became flawed. When we decided we wanted another child, we opted for interuterine insemination. This entailed giving myself daily injections to stimulate multiple egg development. I also had to go to the doctor's every morning so I could get a "trigger shot" to force my ovulation. Everything was timed, practically to the second, and it was important for Steve to plan for this. He needed to be with me at a particular point in the procedure to produce a sperm specimen. Planning was crucial.

During one of my visits to the doctor, Steve got a phone call from his mother. She said that Steve's sister, who was pregnant, was in labor but there were complications. She insisted that Steve come home to be with his sister, even though it was an eight-hour drive! I was lying on the exam table at the doctor's office at this point, with Steve relaying his mother's end of the conversation to me, and of course I assumed he'd tell her there was no way he could leave—he needed to be with me for *his* part of the interuterine insemination.

And that is when I had my defining moment, because right then and there, Steve made his choice—and it was to leave me to be with his sister.

I realized that in spite of his saying how much he loved me and wanted another child with me, I would never come first with him. Knowing how important it was for us to carefully plan for the hoped-for pregnancy, Steve still let spontaneity rule his actions. I couldn't believe he left me lying there. When he returned from witnessing the birth of his sister's child, he found I'd changed the locks on the house. Our marriage, as far as I was concerned, was over.

DR. STERN

~

The phrase "Physician, heal thyself" has special meaning for Dr. Stern. A self-proclaimed "fixer" since childhood, Dr. Stern initially tried to solve the problems in her marriage by using an age-old technique: ignoring them. It was only after she realized that some problems can't be fixed that she was able to emotionally heal and move on with her life.

Today, the forty-seven-year-old physician enjoys helping other people in her successful medical practice. She resides in an affluent community in Long Island New York, with her second husband and two children.

I always have had a need to fix things, to make things better, even as a child. I guess I've always been very mature for my age. My parents' relationship was not great. My father is a functioning alcoholic, and on occasion he would throw things and get angry. I remember my mother asking for money and my father saying no. I think that's part of what spearheaded me to want a career where I could support myself. Watching my parents' relationship made me want to succeed and do well. They were good parents, and I always felt I could talk to them. But their relationship was something that I knew I did not want to emulate in my own marriage.

Getting married and having children was important to me, but I also wanted to focus on my career. Once I decided that I wanted to be a physician, there was no stopping me. I was extremely motivated, but I also was nervous about the length of time it would take to establish a medical career—I was afraid that it would be difficult to meet someone or that by the time I did, I would be too old to have children.

While I was completing my residency I thought I might meet another physician in whom I could be interested, but that wasn't in the cards for me. So I did what so many others seemed to be doing: I placed an ad in the personals, and that is how Josh and I met.

The funny thing is that Josh actually responded to my girlfriend's ad, but she wasn't interested in dating him. But I was interested—I thought he was cute.

I was twenty-six, and Josh was thirty-one when we started dating. We quickly became aware that we had a lot in common. He had a Maltese—my favorite breed of dogs. He owned a Manhattan deli, and my father's sideline business was a food concession stand. I'm Jewish, and so was Josh. I liked him a lot—he was very pleasant, and I enjoyed his company. And he was up front about his past problems with substance abuse—he assured me it was in the past.

Josh said he was really crazy about me, and I had never experienced this kind of love and attention from any man. He seemed to be my perfect companion—someone with whom I could share my life with and who would take care of me. Josh and I married three years later and went to Israel for our honeymoon. Even though his parents were both Holocaust survivors, while we were in Israel, we visited several of his second and third cousins. All during our marriage, we spent a lot of time with his parents and family members. I remember thinking how nice it was to become part of his family—even as I realized I was ignoring the red flags.

I began to realize that Josh had an addictive personality. When I was pregnant with our first child, I discovered that Josh was betting large amounts of money and had already lost nine hundred dollars. Then I discovered that Josh had forged my name on a credit card application for which the credit amount was eighty thousand dollars.

By the time I discovered it, he'd already charged thousands of dollars. He kept telling me that he needed the money for his business. Even though I recognized the severity of this problem, I wanted to work things out with him.

Then he began taking Quaaludes. Early in our marriage, he'd admitted to me that he had been taking tranquilizers to relax, but now it had escalated to a point that was unacceptable to me. I realized that we had serious problems when I caught myself thinking that I wanted to get on with my life and our life together, but although I could makes plans for my own life, I couldn't do so for Josh—or for our life together.

It was even becoming difficult for us to socialize with friends. Josh had always been introverted, but he was becoming even more so. I can recall feeling very embarrassed at times, particularly when we went to synagogue functions, and he would tell off-color jokes and be very sarcastic and then would retreat for the rest of the evening. It was probably due to nervousness, but he seemed to lack basic social skills.

Between his drug issues and our financial situation, I started seeing a therapist—I wanted someone to explain to me how I could fix my marriage. My psychiatrist, however, recommended that I leave Josh, which I did not want to do. And so that was the end of my therapy.

Things continued to get worse with Josh. He worked at his deli business from five in the morning until three in the afternoon. Because he got home much earlier in the day than I did, he had plenty of time to take his Quaaludes without my catching him.

Our children—we had two by this time—were four and six years old, but Josh wasn't exactly a hands-on kind of father, even in his best moments; when he was high on whatever drugs he was taking, I couldn't trust him to be alone with the kids. In fact, I couldn't trust him to do anything—he couldn't pay bills; he couldn't help around the house or with the children; he couldn't give me emotional support. He had nothing to offer to our relationship and even less to offer to our children. One day, our youngest son, who was somewhat of a wild and hyperactive child, had somehow got his tongue stuck onto the back of our dehumidifier. Josh was so out of it, he didn't know what to do. Luckily we had live in help at the time who promptly knew to call EMS. But I knew that Josh was becoming increasingly useless. And I couldn't fix that.

My defining moment came when I finally realized that we had been living this way for ten years. I wanted out of this marriage.

At first Josh was okay with my decision to seek a divorce, but that may have been because his mind was clouded by drugs. Once he was thinking clearly, he became defensive. I think that part of that anger stemmed from the fact that he knew that my mother had stood by my father, even with his alcohol addiction, so Josh expected that we would recreate the same scenario. Of course he didn't want our marriage to end—it was a great situation for him. He absolutely refused to leave the house, and he began doing things to annoy me, like camping out in the middle of the living room. Josh's downfall, however, came when he tried one trick that backfired on him. Thanks to the help of the local police, (who installed a hidden camera in our home to capture Josh's actions), we found out Josh was taping my phone calls. Josh was subsequently arrested for illegal wire-tapping. After that, getting a divorce was easier.

Fortunately, my experience with Josh didn't negatively impact my opinion of men, in general. I realized not all men were like Josh, and it wasn't long after I started searching Yahoo! Personals and began dating again. I met a wonderful man to whom I am now happily married. He is truly an equal and loving partner on whom I always can rely.

NATALIE

~

Natalie believes that "the one" exists for her somewhere, but after two failed relationships, she's careful about assigning that title to another man. Now forty-one years old, she lives with her son in Tucson, Arizona, where she is a massage therapist at day and a bartender at night.

———————

*M*y dad was a very attractive man, and that eventually caused him problems, because he had many affairs while he and my mother were married; he couldn't seem to turn down the ladies. But when I was growing up, I always hoped to find a guy who was as handsome as my dad. And I did find that guy when I met Ken. Once we started dating, we had sex almost right away, and I became pregnant. Because I was still in high school and was frightened, I had an abortion, and Ken and I eventually split up. This was very traumatic for me because I thought I really loved him; I really thought he was the "one."

While I was growing up I never really thought about getting married. Sure, I wanted a boyfriend, but marriage didn't seem to be part of the equation. I guess that's because my mom and dad never were in a partnership that I wanted to emulate. And after Ken, I thought I'd never find that kind of love again.

And then I met Antonio. I had asked God to send me Antonio Banderas, and he sent me a guy who not only had the same first name but who also looked just like Antonio Banderas! People would actually stop him in the street and ask him for his autograph, thinking he was the movie star.

Antonio and I met on my thirty-fourth birthday, when he came into the bar where I worked with a couple of his friends. The night he came in happened to be gay night, but he was unaware of that fact. But once he became aware of the fact that it was gay night, he stuck closely by my side. Antonio and I struck up a conversation and hit it off immediately. Soon, we were dating, and I'm sure people thought we had very little in common. He was reserved and quiet; I'm a fireball and run my mouth a mile a minute. But when we were together, I felt a kind of spiritual connection with him.

As time went on, however, I found out that he was a talented con man. Turned out that he was mysterious for a reason I didn't understand until about five months later. By that time in our relationship, we were living together—and then I found out that he had a wife and three children. His wife had seen Antonio driving my car, took down the license plate number, found out where I was living, and slipped a note under my door. In her note, she let me know that she was married to Antonio. She didn't want him back; she just wanted him to take responsibility for his kids. When I confronted Antonio, he tried to convince me that his wife was a little crazy and that he'd never mentioned her because she was no longer important to him.

I wanted to believe him, so I gave him another chance with our relationship. I insisted he include his children in our life together, which he did, and then I became pregnant with our child. It seemed like we were turning into one big, happy family. When I was four months pregnant, Antonio went to Italy to attend his cousin's wedding. It was just after September 11th, and I was terrified for him to fly, but he insisted he would be safe. He was right about that—he got to Italy without any problems—but once he got over there, he decided to stay. I was sure he would come home—all his things were at my apartment—but after about a month of trying to reach him (he wouldn't take my calls), I realized he didn't plan to return.

When my son—*our* son—was eighteen months old, I saw Antonio walking down the street. He didn't see us, though, and I didn't call out to him. You might think I had a defining moment that let me know that Antonio wasn't "the one" when he left me during my pregnancy or when he made no attempt to contact me about his child. But it wasn't.

My defining moment came when I saw Antonio on the street, and I remembered his deceit and abandonment. And I suddenly realized how lucky I was to have him out of my life. I found out recently that Antonio's mother conceived him during an extra-marital affair, so deceit was something that seemed bred into Antonio. His mother also gave Antonio to his grandmother when he was a baby so she could raise him, so Antonio learned about abandonment at an early age. He never had a father role model. I guess that explains a lot.

But I don't want my son growing up with Antonio as his role model; I don't want him to continue that cycle of deceit and abandonment. Max is four now, and although it breaks my heart when he asks about his father, I just tell him that his father had to go away and can't be with us. We do all right with just the two of us, but I'm still hoping that one day, I will find "the one."

PAULA

~

When Paula met the man who would become her husband, he seemed to embody all the qualities she wanted in a man. He was charming and handsome, but most importantly, they shared a strong spiritual faith. Paula was married for nearly twenty years before she realized that her husband's definition of being a good Christian was vastly different from her own. Now divorced for six years, fifty-four-year-old Paula lives in Las Vegas, Nevada, where she works as a buyer for a large department store.

My parents provided me with a very secure upbringing. They were terrific people, and to me, their relationship was idyllic. They seemed very much like the Cleavers from the old TV show *Leave It to Beaver*—they were always really nice to each other but were never overly affectionate. When I was a young girl, I yearned for a relationship like my parents, except I wanted my relationship to have more physical affection and romance—like Claire and Cliff Huxtable from *The Cosby Show*. They always appeared friendly, warm and playful.

So when I met Phil, I looked for these qualities. I met him in college when I was twenty-five and he was twenty-eight. We were both attending school and we were older than most college kids because I was traveling in a play and he was touring off-Broadway and in Europe. When I first saw him in my communication class, I thought he was attractive, elegant, and mature. What I especially liked about him, though, was that he was Christian—it was (and still is) very important to me that my partner have a strong spiritual faith. I thought Phil was honest and had a lot of integrity. It wasn't long before I was in love with him.

I'd hoped my parents would love him, too, but they didn't like him; they said he was too dogmatic. Phil liked to discuss his Christian beliefs with my parents, but if they questioned something he said, Phil would get angry and defensive. This caused a lot of problems. This wasn't the only time that Phil's anger was an issue. He lived with a nice couple—a pastor and his wife—who took me aside one day to tell me about their concern for Phil. They said they had suggested counseling for him to deal with his anger, but he'd refused. They wanted me to know he wasn't dealing with his problem.

When Phil asked me to marry him, however, I accepted. That little voice in my head was telling me I should have reservations about him, based on what the pastor and his wife had told me about his anger; but I ignored it. We had a lovely wedding—even though I walked down the aisle filled with apprehension.

Shortly after we got married, we started traveling around the country because Phil was a professional singer and speaker, as well as a news anchor for a TV network. We seemed to have a great marriage—until I began to notice that he was exhibiting his anger more frequently. He wasn't abusive to me, but he would get angry about trivial things. Long before the term "road rage" became popular, Phil was the poster boy. He would drive like a maniac—cutting people off, weaving at high speeds between cars, honking his horn and yelling at other drivers. If I asked him why he was yelling, he'd say it was the other driver's fault. Phil would never take responsibility for his actions.

Although Phil had a successful career as a TV anchorman, he longed for more. Eventually, he became involved with a Christian-based cable station, where he had his own TV show—he was the singing pastor. His TV audience was massive, and as the show's ratings improved, I noticed he started to get more and more narcissistic. He felt that because God had blessed him with an incredible voice and the capacity to be on a cable show, he could do anything he wanted to do. Apparently, as I found out later, this included having an affair.

My defining moment came when I got a phone call from a friend, who told me that Phil's affair was common knowledge around the cable station. She was torn over whether to tell me, but she didn't want me to overhear someone gossiping about it.

I'd overlooked Phil's narcissism and anger issues, but having an affair was something I couldn't overlook. To make matters even worse, when I confronted Phil, his response was to tell me that "lots of TV pastors have affairs," so why was I making a big deal out of it? I couldn't believe that this man who seemed to have such strong Christian values now considered himself above the morals of society. He admitted to me that he'd had at least fifteen affairs that he could remember—the first one started on the day after our wedding. Suddenly, divorcing Phil was my only option. It wasn't easy for me, though. My world had completely fallen apart. For several months after learning the truth, I was in a complete funk—I'd lost everything: my financial security, my status in the community, and my husband (who, I discovered, I'd never really had in the first place).

Eventually, however, I began to heal. I became involved with a women's support group, and I found out that helping other women was helping me too. I began to rebuild a new, stable life for myself. I know there will be bends and dips in the road ahead, but now I can actually see the sun rising over the horizon.

GINA

~

Gina tends to see the good in most people, even when her instincts might warn her against it. After suffering a traumatic experience as a college student, Gina became involved with—and eventually married—a man who seemed to offer her protection, but this only blinded her to his true character. Now twenty-eight and divorced after only five months of marriage, Gina feels at peace with herself and is happy with her decisions. She is a scientist who recently moved back into her parents' home in Mystic, Connecticut.

I grew up in a non-traditional Italian household—it was non-traditional because my mom was the boss of the household; my father was easygoing and gentle, and he took on more of a "mothering" role. My parents' marriage is a wonderful model for a great relationship. They have been married for thirty-three years and are each other's best friend. They really seem to enjoy being with each other.

When I was a young girl and would fantasize about my future husband, I always pictured someone who could be my best friend. I wanted a man who was nurturing and kind, so I could have a relationship like the one my parents have.

Chip and I started dating when I was twenty-two years old and he was twenty-seven years. I was attracted to him because he was very handsome but also rather gruff looking. His rough exterior was attractive to me, though, because I thought it meant that he could offer me protection. And I needed to feel protected because of an incident that occurred when I was a freshman in college—I was date-raped by a fellow student. It was an incredibly traumatic experience, and I went for counseling for several months.

I was still suffering with post traumatic stress and sometimes the weirdest triggers would just affect me but as I got to know Chip, who was initially supportive and sympathic, as our relationship continued, the fact that I was raped definitely played a negative effect on our relationship. I had a hard time being able to be touched and be present in my body. So I did my homework and found a therapist who would help bring me back into my body and helped me to be less anxious. However, anyone recovering from rape knows that they have to take it one day at a time.

At the time that I met Chip, I still wasn't completely healed. I had just graduated and moved to a new town to start my new life as a teacher—Chip was a teacher at the same school where I'd gotten a job. I liked the fact that he was five years older than I was because I thought that age difference also meant he would be protective toward me. Shortly after we started dating, however, I realized that the roughness was not only on Chip's exterior; it was also how he was internally.

Chip's mother was a very soft and sweet woman who had a very loving relationship with Chip, but his father was quite the opposite. His father had been diagnosed as bi-polar several years ago and also was an alcoholic and was constanly drinking and was quite unpredictable. Sometimes, if I went over to see his parents without Chip, his father would purposely answer the door, wearing only his underwear and he was often saying inappropriate comments to me or making sexual references to me. He was also very frightening because he had a huge weapons collection in the house. In fact, the first time Chip ever took me over to his parent's house, when I went to sit down on their couch, I sat on top of some loose bullets!

Chip often seemed like two completely different people. One moment he was romantic, funny, and great to be with; the next moment he was terrifying. His anger would be so overwhelming that I would freeze and try to be very, very small. As our relationship progressed, Chip started to become extremely rough during sex. He also became verbally abusive, telling me that everything and anything that went wrong was entirely my fault. But then his personality would flip, and he was charming and romantic. Even with his Jekyll and Hyde personality, I desperately wanted to marry him; I was foolishly in love. I loved him for who he was, and I loved him for what I believed he was capable of being.

After we'd been dating for four years, Chip asked me to marry him. We'd moved in together the previous month, so I knew marriage was a probable option, but Chip was very romantic about it. And even though I knew I'd be accepting "Mr. Hyde" as well as "Dr. Jekyll," I agreed to marry him. For a few weeks after our engagement, Chip seemed happy. Then we attended a cousin's wedding in Vermont, a three-hour drive away. When we arrived at the little inn where we would stay that night and began to change into our clothes for the church, all hell broke loose. Chip was furious because I hadn't packed the shirt he'd wanted to wear.

Later, when we were together with my family, Chip totally ignored me. Even worse, he wouldn't talk to anyone in my family either. I was so embarrassed. Although we'd planned to stay in Vermont the entire weekend, we ended up leaving right after the wedding. Chip screamed at me for the entire three-hour drive back home. He said that I made him look like a fool in front of my family and, as always, everything was my fault. And because I was fearful and trapped in the car with him, I had to endure his behavior.

This incident should have been a serious red flag for me, but Chip had recently started going to counseling to deal with his anger issues, so I told myself that his behavior that weekend had been a momentary lapse.

And so we got married. It was only four months into our marriage when I realized that Chip was not the "one." *My defining moment was painfully obvious: Chip came home one day and simply announced that he didn't think that he ever really loved me. In fact, he went on, the only reason he had married me was because he needed my strength to help him to improve his life. Furthermore, even though he was not in love with me, he wanted to stay married because he liked his life as it was.*

I was devastated. Part of me wanted to believe that he was saying these things because he was taking medication as part of his therapy to control his anger. But the more logical part of me realized that the man who was "the one" for me would not say the things that Chip had just said.

We didn't immediately split up—I suppose I hoped we might somehow save our marriage—but from that point on, he never touched me again. Chip also stopped doing anything around the house—I managed all of the finances and all of the day-to-day stuff. But I was totally crushed; I couldn't believe that this was the man I'd married just four months ago. We had a beautiful new house; I had a fantastic job; and we were still newlyweds. Things should have been great. But now, in that one defining moment, our marriage had become a sham.

Still, I thought maybe it would help to enter counseling together, so we made an appointment to jointly see his therapist. In the end, though, all we gained from the therapy session was a realization that we should separate. In fact, when Chip and I left the therapist's office, Chip reaffirmed that he no longer wanted to work on the marriage. He also told me that he really never even liked me, and he couldn't wait to be away from me. My only thought at that time was that at least he was telling me all this in a calm voice. And I felt a sense of peace myself, in that I would never have to endure his incredible rage ever again.

I know now that had I not been raped, I would have never been attracted to a guy like Chip. It was his rough exterior that made me think he would keep me safe, when I should have recognized that his rough exterior only mirrored his true self. But when all is said and done, I have learned that I am stronger than I ever realized; I am equipped to prevail. I experienced two significant events in my life and I have been blessed with incredible friends and family and I am just surrounded by love. My family and friends are there to carry me when I need to be carried, so that I know everything will be okay.

Once our divorce became final, I decided to throw out my wedding album. The one picture that I did keep, is a photograph of all of the women in my life. All of my girlfriends that came from across the country to attend the wedding, as well as my mother, sister, my aunt and grandmother—all of these dynamic women are all together in one photograph and every time I look at that picture, I know that I am looking at my safety net.

BRITTANY

~

Thirty-one-year-old Brittany was certain her life was on the right track. She'd found the perfect guy, and she was sure their life together would be amazing. Today, she considers herself fortunate that her "perfect" guy broke off their engagement. As she later learned, she could soar much higher without him. Now contentedly single, Brittany lives in Washington, DC and, is an ordained minister.

I was diagnosed with clinical depression at age nineteen. Although my depression was apparent to me much earlier, no one in the family wanted to acknowledge it. My parents couldn't accept that something was wrong with me because they felt it would indicate some inadequacy in them. Our family was well off, financially, but my parents had virtually no communication between them. My mom was a hard-working financial wizard on Wall Street, whereas my dad was more laid back. He also was an alcoholic. Neither of them was prepared to accept the responsibility of being a parent, so I had a nanny from the day I was born until I turned sixteen years old. Becky, my nanny, was a special person in my life; I loved her like a mom.

When I was eleven, I started gaining weight because I was eating to make myself feel better emotionally. I think this was the beginning of my battle with depression. By the time I went away to college, my depression had become more obvious. I was living in a dorm and the lack of privacy caused me to become more and more withdrawn. Finally, I went to the college mental health center, where I was evaluated and prescribed antidepressants. It was about this time that my parents told me they were divorcing. My mom and dad were unable to cope with my cries for help because they were both reeling from their own breakup. I decided then that the best thing for me to do would be to visit my old nanny, Becky, who was now retired and living in Aruba. She was always someone to whom I could go to for nurturing and a listening ear. And so I planned to visit her over Christmas break. I invited my roommate Susan to come with me, and she asked if her brother Jeff could come along too. Jeff was older—he was working on his master's degree—and he was very attractive: tall, blond, and well built.

I had a wonderful time in Aruba. It was great to see Becky again, but it was also fun to be there with Jeff. There was a lot of drinking and a lot of fun, and Jeff became very affectionate with me, which I enjoyed! I was ready to have an adult relationship, and Jeff seemed ready to have a relationship with me.

On the way back home, I couldn't stop dreaming up scenarios about how our life together would be. Jeff was smart and he wanted to be a dentist; he had specific goals. I was sure we would be perfect together. Soon, he graduated and moved back home to Rhode Island, about an hour away from me. I often visited him there, and his parents and I got along very well. Then Jeff decided to return to Boston, where I was still in school, to attend dental school. I was so happy—we spent all our free time together, and my depression seemed under control. Everything was going so well with our relationship, in fact, that we decided to move in together.

By this time I had graduated and had found a job in Boston so that we could stay together. And because our future now seemed set, we decided to get engaged. I was so excited and in love with him. In my mind, we had the perfect partnership. Four months later, however, he suddenly dropped a bombshell: He told me that he didn't think that we should be engaged anymore. I was shocked. There'd been no indication from Jeff that he was unhappy with our engagement.

I recently had developed irritable bowel disease and had lost a great deal of weight, (both issues due to my depression and medication problems), so Jeff explained that these issues had made him wonder if this was the right time to get married. When I started crying, he said we didn't have to break up altogether; we could continue to live together.

His family was coming to have dinner with us—it was Thanksgiving—and when they arrived, they learned the engagement was over. Susan, who was still my best friend as well as Jeff's sister, was really upset and confronted Jeff about this decision. But he couldn't offer a concrete explanation on why he wanted to call off the engagement.

I probably should have made a clean break with him, but I was devastated by the idea of losing him. So we continued to live together. I told myself that Jeff was just going through a phase, and he eventually would change his mind.

A few months later, Jeff said he was going home to visit his parents. I couldn't leave my job, so I told him I'd join him there on the weekend. Imagine my surprise when I got a call from Susan later that day, telling me that Jeff had brought a girl home with him! She said I should still come for the weekend as planned, and although I knew it would be awkward, I couldn't let Jeff go without a fight. So for that weekend, we all were in the house together: his parents, his sister, Jeff and the girl (whose name was Audrey), and me. As I found out, Audrey was completely unaware that Jeff was seeing anyone else—let alone that we had been engaged and were still living together. That weekend, with everyone at his parents' house, was one of the saddest and weirdest times of my life. I don't know what Jeff was thinking, but he didn't seem at all embarrassed that I was there. I later learned he had told Audrey that I was one of Susan's friends—which, of course, was true, but he left out the part about our having been engaged. Finally, the weekend was over and I returned to Boston, completely in tears during the entire trip. Jeff and Audrey drove back to Boston together. I didn't know what I was going to do, but I knew I had to do something. When Jeff got back, he walked into our apartment as if nothing unusual had happened. I couldn't believe he was so unfeeling.

It was around this time that I was practicing for a twenty-six mile marathon. This was my first marathon, and it would be a great accomplishment if I could complete this run. I took all the pent-up anger and agitation that I felt toward Jeff, and I just let the pavement have it. As sweat poured off my face with every stride, I just let the momentum of my feelings catapult me to the finish line. And I made it! I actually completed the race. This gave me a great feeling of accomplishment; it was better than anything I'd ever experienced. *And it was then that I experienced my defining moment: I realized that I must take back control of my life. I had completed the marathon, so I knew that I could do anything.*

So I told Jeff that I was going back to Rhode Island to figure out what I wanted to do with my life. Not surprisingly, he showed no emotion over my decision. But this time, his uncaring attitude didn't faze me. I had my life back.

Shortly after I left Boston, Jeff married Audrey. There was a time when I would have been sent into a spiraling depression over that news, but when Susan phoned me, I only laughed.

Since this experience I soon learned to give myself positive affirmations. I suddenly began to ask myself what I wanted for me. I realized it was divinity school. And so I pursued my desires to be a source to help others through my ministry. I am able to be a real person's minister. I curse, I have premarital sex and I live a true authentic life. I considered myself lucky to have gotten out of my relationship with Jeff. I am my own person, and I like who I am. And my life is getting more energized every day.

ROSE

~

Rose admits that she is still trying to recapture her inner strength—strength that her twelve-year marriage to a much-older man essentially destroyed. Today, she is free from her ex-husband's manipulative control and is once again dreaming big dreams for herself and her three children. Now forty-three years old, Rose teaches at a preschool in Milwaukee, Wisconsin.

I didn't date a lot as a teenager. I always wanted to be more popular with the boys, but it never happened. My dad was a minister, so our family moved frequently—every few years or so—when he was assigned to a new parish. And I guess because I was so often "the new girl," it was hard to make friends, especially with boys. I never had any real expectations of love. My parents had a comfortable relationship, but it wasn't like they were outwardly romantic—at least, not in front of me—so I didn't have the idea of an ideal relationship in my head.

I was twenty-two when I met Brian, and he was thirty-five. He was working at a convenience store near my house, and I'd stopped in to get some milk. I didn't pay much attention to him, other than noticing he was moderately attractive. He also had cerebral palsy that affected the left side of his body. But he apparently paid attention to me, because he called me the following weekend. (He saw my name on my credit card and looked me up in the phone book.) I was surprised to hear from him—we hadn't even had a conversation in the store—but he seemed nice on the phone, so I agreed to have dinner with him. That first date was fun—we went to a Pizza Hut, so it was nothing fancy, but Brian seemed like a great guy.

We continued dating, and I was really awed by him. He had a photographic memory, and he seemed to know so much about lots of different things. It really was kind of a parent/child relationship, because he was so much older than I was, and he would be very nurturing.

Soon, Brian asked me to move in with him. In my previous relationships, I had never felt like making that kind of commitment. But with Brian, I had no second thoughts at all. We moved in together, and shortly after that, he asked me to marry him. There wasn't any great passion with him, but I thought he'd be a good provider, and I think I fell in love with him. So eight months after we met, Brian and I got married. We had a small church wedding and a simple reception.

We'd had sex before we got married, and it had been good. But after we got married, it wasn't good at all. Brian basically controlled our sex life—he dictated when we were going to have sex and when we weren't. I guess because of our age difference, my libido was stronger than his, but there hadn't been any problems before we were married, so I couldn't figure it out. The amount of sex dropped off immediately, the day we were married. At first, I blamed myself, thinking maybe I wasn't pretty or sexy anymore. I began to have a lot of self-doubts.

We had only been married a couple weeks when it seemed like Brian was getting progressively angry with me. It happened a lot. Sometimes he would just yell at me in the middle of a parking lot or in a store. We didn't really have fights out in public; he would just yell at me, and then I would tell him, "You can't talk to me like that. It's not okay for you to talk to me that way." And then that was the end of it.

Brian also began to experience anger issues surrounding his cerebral palsy disability. He had been teased as a child and picked on constantly at school, and he was still angry about it because his family had never protected him.

Around this time we had our first child, a son. Brian was not really involved with our son. He even claimed he couldn't even change a diaper because of his disability. He also claimed he couldn't help around the house—he never cooked a meal or helped with the laundry. So with a new baby, I had a lot more to handle on my own.

After we had our second child, a daughter, I stopped doing so much around the house because he refused to help. I had full responsibility of the children and the household, and I also had two outside jobs. Even though this time was very stressful for me and I should have seen the red flags that showed the end of our relationship, I still allowed myself to get pregnant again.

By this time I found myself secretly wishing that Brian would die—I thought that was the only way I'd ever be free of him. He'd gained a lot of weight in the ten years we'd been married, and I would think that if he didn't take care of himself, he'd die—and then I'd think, "That would be a good thing!" I was so unhappy, I sometimes wished that I would die, too, but then I realized my children would have only Brian, and he was a terrible father

It was around this time when a very disturbing situation occurred. The two older kids were being rowdy and loud while Brian was watching TV. Instead of asking them to settle down, he picked up two books and threw a book at each of them. The corner of the book hit my daughter under her eye, leaving a golf-ball-sized contusion. She had a black eye for months. *That was my defining moment—when I realized that Brian had so little concern for his own children that he would throw things at them rather than communicate, and that when he wounded one of them, he felt she deserved it.*

We got divorced, and I started to rebuild my life as a single mom with three kids. Although Brian had shown little interest in his children when we were married, he did seem to become a better father after the divorce, taking the kids to his house on a regular basis. Then one day, my older daughter, who was about eleven at the time, told me something shocking: She told me that Brian was touching her in a bad way and that he had actually tried to penetrate her. Once she realized I believed her and wasn't mad about it, she recounted numerous graphic events that took place when Brian had her at his place, including how he made her watch pornography. I immediately got on the phone with Child Protective Services, and Brian was arrested. I soon learned that not only was my husband—her father molesting my daughter, but that her brother—my son was molesting her as well. In fact my husband and son were in the same jail at the same time.

Fortunately, my daughter is okay now; she's a pretty strong person. I wish I could have spared her that experience, but I had no idea that Brian was like that. I realized—too late—that Brian liked girls much younger than he was. This should have been obvious, I guess; I am thirteen years younger than Brian.

It's been six years since my divorce, and I am finally starting to feel better about myself. My children and I have a long way to go before our healing is complete, but we are standing on our own feet and have the support of each other and our family and friends.

SERENA

~

After two failed marriages, thirty-eight-year-old Serena hopes she's found the man with whom she can be happy. Circumstances currently keep them apart, but she is looking forward to the future. Serena lives with her two children in Manhattan, where she works as an clothing designer.

---

*W*hen I was a teenager, I wanted to get married young. I thought my marriage would be happy-go-lucky, and I would have children and a husband who loved me. I always expected I would live a life like my parents, who are still happily married after forty-five years. Unfortunately, my first marriage was unhappy. I was miserable during this marriage and secretly looking for someone who would give me some attention.

I met Carlos, the man who would become my second husband, when I was working at a bank, and he was a customer. He had beautiful brown eyes and appeared to be very soft-spoken, kind, and charming. He must have been attracted to me, too, because we exchanged work numbers and made a date to get together. There was just one problem: I was still married to my first husband. Carlos confided in me that he was unhappily married and had a three-year-old son.

Initially, our "dates" consisted of going to parking lots, since we were both still married. Our favorite spot was a hospital rooftop parking lot. At times the construction workers would applaud us after we finished our sexual escapades. We would also meet at playgrounds. I had a three-year-old daughter, so Carlos and I would take the kids on play dates to the park, just so we could be together.

I knew my husband was having affairs. First of all, he was hardly ever home, but he also left condom wrappers and girl's hair clips in the back of his car. He never knew I was seeing someone because he was never around. Soon after I started dating Carlos, my husband moved out and Carlos moved in. We were married two years later.

During the first years of marriage, everything was going great. I became pregnant and had our son. Carlos was a good father and was involved with all the kids.

After a few years, though, Carlos started to change. I noticed that he was very involved with watching porn. One day I went to see him at his office, and I saw that he had a porn screensaver on his computer. I was mortified, especially because one of his employees had also seen it. But Carlos just shrugged his shoulders and pretended it wasn't important. I just couldn't believe that my husband looked at porn in his professional office.

Eventually, he started watching porn at home. At first, I didn't say anything because I thought it would make him happy, but he wanted me to watch with him, and it didn't excite me at all. I remember wondering why he needed to watch porn for sexual fulfillment. Wasn't I enough? I began to feel so inadequate, so unable to fulfill his needs, that I even brought someone else into our bedroom for him. I felt like I needed to do that to spice things up, because I saw there was no "spice" left between us. So I hired a prostitute. Having a threesome actually made an exciting difference. But although I enjoyed myself at the time, by the next morning I had second thoughts about it. I didn't really want to share my husband. I realized this when we found the prostitute's comb on our nightstand, and Carlos picked it up and smelled it. He said, "I still smell her," For some reason, that offended me, so I told Carlos that we would never invite someone else into our bedroom again. He shrugged and didn't seem too concerned, but as our marriage progressed, I realized that I was always trying to please him—he never showed any consideration for my needs. Every morning when Carlos was in the shower, I would provide oral sex which he called his "Breakfast of Champions." Again, he never considered if my needs were being met, and I didn't question it because I felt it was my duty to please my husband. We went on like this for thirteen years.

My defining moment came when Carlos told me one day that he just didn't love me, and he hadn't loved me for the last eight years.

I was stunned. I had spent all my time trying to please him. I asked him, "If you no longer love me, why do you let me perform oral sex every morning?" And he said, "While you do that, at least I don't have to look at your face. I can fantasize that you are someone else." Just imagine what that did to my self-esteem. I have never felt so crushed. I told Carlos to get out of the house, and he left without any argument.

During our separation, I had some financial problems. Then I developed major depression and had several anxiety attacks that were so bad, I couldn't even go to my job. I had been an established employee who had been financially stable up until then. Carlos had emotionally crippled me.

A few months ago I met a new man at a car dealership, and we started dating. Unfortunately, he was recently incarcerated for petty larceny. He is due for release soon, and I am looking forward to the time when we can be together again.

I'm still trying to get divorced from Carlos, but he is fighting me for custody of our son. Carlos says it's because he doesn't want our son to be around someone who has been in jail. He seems to be forcing me to choose between my son and my boyfriend. I am trying to get on with my life, but I still don't know what I am going to do.

CHELSEA

~

Chelsea's long-term relationship with an older man taught her lessons she couldn't possibly have learned in any of her classes as a third-year college student. Although the end of the relationship was painful, she has come out of it a much wiser and more self-assured person. Currently a psychology major at a local college, twenty-two-year-old Chelsea lives at home with her mother in Grand Rapids, Michigan.

When I was a child, I thought of love as a fairy tale thing. I pictured myself as meeting someone, falling in love, and being together without any problems. My older sister was in a relationship with a wonderful guy; it seemed like they had a great relationship, and I always wanted to have that kind of idyllic relationship.

I'd known Dave for a long time because he was friends with my older brother, but I didn't like him when I was younger—even though I was a child, I thought he was crude. Then, when I was eighteen, I happened to bump into Dave while I was vacationing with some friends, and my childhood opinion of him immediately changed! He was almost twenty-seven then and very good-looking. He also was real funny and had a very outgoing personality. I found his sense of humor and his personality very appealing.

We decided to keep in touch after the vacation. We would go to clubs every weekend or, because it was still summer, we'd hang out at the beach during the day. Dave was a real estate investor and was doing quite well, so he could afford to take me places. We were always going out to dinner or doing something fun. After dating for several months, Dave said that he wanted an exclusive relationship. I was a little surprised, because I thought we already had an exclusive relationship!

The funny thing though, was, that Dave did not like to take me around his friends. I know now that he had a lot of insecurities as far as his friends were concerned; his friends always thought that I was too young for him. But I never felt the age difference. We had great conversations, and we had so much in common. We loved the same music, loved doing the same activities. And since I was part African American and Dave was African American, we shared the same culture.

But what should have been a major red flag was something I virtually ignored. Dave was not in a hurry to introduce me to his parents. They would periodically come to see him—they lived out of town—but Dave would never invite me over while they were in town. He would say that because he didn't want to introduce me to them until he was one hundred percent sure about our future together. I tried to understand his viewpoint, but one incident stands out in my memory as being too much for me to accept.

When we'd been dating for about three years, Dave found out that his grandfather was terminally ill and in the hospital. Because Dave had never introduced me to his family, his grandfather thought Dave was still dating Jackie, the girl he had dated for ten years before he and I got together. So when his grandfather asked to see Jackie, rather than tell him that he'd broken up with her, Dave actually brought her to the hospital to see his grandfather—his ex-girlfriend was at the hospital with all of Dave's family!

Jackie became somewhat of an obsession for me. I'd often ask Dave why he hadn't married her when they'd dated for ten years. He'd just say he'd stayed with her because it was "comfortable," but that she was too manipulative.

After the hospital incident, I felt that our relationship began to get a little rocky. Dave wouldn't call when he said he would, and he was always running late. One day, I waited all day to hear from him, but he never called, even though he'd said he would. His explanation was that he had a lot going on at work and had lost track of time.

Then Dave started to become controlling about the way I dressed. He wanted me to be more "toned down" and conservative, but I was in college so I dressed like any college student. Dave also started going on trips with one of his guy friends. I didn't mind that he did this, except at the beginning of our relationship, he always took me along on his trips.

More red flags kept waving, but I was so sure that Dave was right for me that I didn't see them. Dave and I had the same type of cell phones, and we often picked up each other's phone by mistake. One day I accidentally picked up his phone, and when I flipped it open, there was a text message that read, "Hey, honey, don't forget to call me tonight." When I confronted Dave, he said that it was from his cousin.

I was sure it was another woman; I just didn't know who it was. Later that night, Dave must have felt guilty about lying because he confessed that the text message had been from Jackie. He said that after he took her to see his grandfather, they'd realized they could still be friends. That was Dave's explanation of the whole situation, even when Jackie began calling his apartment late at night. I told Dave numerous times that his so-called friendship with Jackie made me feel very uncomfortable, but he said I was being silly.

I began to suspect that he was secretly seeing her again. We would argue about her, over and over again. I became so obsessed with this that I got to the point where I was looking through his phone, just to see if I would find something. But if I did find something—a text from Jackie or a record of a phone call—I would probably accept the excuses he gave for why he'd been talking to her. I was still intent on making him the one!

As the relationship progressed, however, my self-esteem began to drop. I didn't feel good about myself at all; I didn't feel pretty anymore. I was constantly comparing myself to other women, particularly to women who were closer to Dave's age and were already finished with school and into their careers. And I resented the fact that Dave continued to make room for someone else—Jackie—to come between us. Because of my suspicions about his infidelity, I became someone I barely recognized—I constantly searched for "evidence." As luck would have it, I eventually found some.

Dave had gone on another trip with his friends, and because I had driven him to the airport, he'd left his car at my house. I searched his car, thinking maybe I'd find some phone numbers, but what I found was more than I'd bargained for; I found his journal. In it, he compared me unfavorably to another woman he knew. He wrote that if not for the fact that he was tied down with me, he would undoubtedly be with her. Dave also wrote that he knew that I wasn't the one for him, and that's why he hadn't asked me to marry him.

I was livid with anger. I wanted to confront him right then, but I had to wait for several days until he was due back from his trip, which was supposed to be that Wednesday. But Dave didn't come home on Wednesday; he came back the following Saturday. Even though I was so angry about what I'd read in his journal, I was still worried about him when he didn't arrive home when he'd said he would, but his only explanation was that he had mixed up his flight times. Then he asked me to bring him his car.

Once I got to his apartment, I immediately confronted him about the stuff that I'd read in his journal. Of course, Dave was more upset that I read his journal than how I felt about what he wrote. He said that those were just "random" thoughts that he had jotted down.

But even after this, I still stuck around. I tried to develop more trust in Dave, and I kept hoping beyond all hope that things would get better, because I still loved him and still wanted to be with him. I didn't want my fairy tale to end.

I think I knew on some level, though, that I was at the beginning of the end. I had told one of my girlfriends that I would not leave him until he told me he didn't love me anymore. I just didn't have the strength to walk away. I knew in my heart that this relationship was all wrong for me, but I just couldn't walk away.

I finally had my defining moment when Dave and I were faced with a life-altering situation: My period was late, so I thought that I was pregnant. When I told Dave, his first words were, "What woman will ever want me in the future if I have a kid?"

That is when I finally got it. I finally realized that Dave did not love me, nor was he ever going to love me. And because I finally accepted this fact, I was able to immediately cease all contact with him. Just like that. Soon after, I found out that I was not pregnant. I decided that the whole experience had been a blessing in disguise.

I have learned a lot about myself because of my relationship with Dave. I may be young, but I feel I have matured. I know that I will have many more experiences before I settle down, but I know that in the future, I will be smarter and will protect myself emotionally.

PEGGY

When Peggy dropped out of college to get married, she was certain it was the right decision. Her marriage, she was sure, would be for life. Instead, it lasted for thirty years before she realized that her husband was not the man she thought she married. Now fifty-eight years old and living in Shreveport, Louisiana, Peggy is involved in local politics.

I grew up in what might be thought of as an unusual family situation. Our entire family lived under one roof—my parents, siblings, aunts, uncles, cousins, and grandparents. Mom was a great, accomplished woman who emigrated from Bulgaria and worked in the family business of textiles. My father tended to be verbally abusive, so I learned I could never argue with him. Their relationship with each other was more functional than loving; it's not something I ever wanted to emulate.

Since we had almost twenty-two people living in our home, it was very difficult to have any quiet time. But when I had some private time during my teenage years, I used to fantasize about how life would be when I grew up and got married. I felt that marriage was for life and that a man would come and sweep me off my feet. He would be romantic, but he also would be a provider and protector.

I didn't go to college to find a husband; it just happened. I met Dan at a homecoming game and thought he was cute—tall and blond, with beautiful ocean-blue eyes. He was a military man who looked great in uniform. He asked me out for coffee, and I found myself really attracted to him; he was very romantic. After only four weeks of dating, Dan suddenly proposed to me—and I accepted. My parents weren't particularly enthused—they thought I was too young, and I hadn't finished my education—but they respected my decision.

Dan's parents planned a rehearsal dinner on the night before the wedding, but I couldn't attend—I was busy packing for Dan's and my move to Houston, where he insisted we relocate after the wedding. When I found out that his parents had invited Dan's former girlfriend to the dinner, I couldn't believe it. My sister told me that Dan spent the entire evening with her and never bothered talking to anyone else—all while I was packing for our move! Later that night, my parents pleaded with me to call off the wedding. They reiterated that I was too young, but I think they saw problems with Dan that I wasn't able to recognize—like his cozying up to his former girlfriend the night before he was to marry me. I should have seen the red flags then, but I guess I was blind.

We had a lovely wedding close to a hundred guests, and despite my parents' reservations, I was excited to be getting married. We postponed our honeymoon, though, because Dan wanted us to get to Houston as soon as possible—we'd both found jobs in the area, although his was thirty miles south of where we lived, and mine was thirty miles north. We lived in a tiny apartment, but I was in love, so it seemed romantic.

I became pregnant during that first year of our marriage, and Dan was fine during my pregnancy. After our daughter was born, however, he became very upset when I would nurse the baby. He admitted he was jealous because the baby took my time away from him. This jealousy flared up again with my next two pregnancies as well; Dan just didn't like me to nurse the babies. He felt that I was not supposed to be shared with the kids; he wanted me all to himself.

Because of his jealousy of his own children, he wasn't a very effective dad. He basically ignored all three daughters, unless he was being verbally abusive to them. Unfortunately, I never stood up for them when Dan abused them; I had never learned how to stand up for myself, and now it seemed like my family history was repeating itself.

For reasons I still don't understand, I stayed in the marriage. At first, I think I felt I needed to protect the children, but later on, I suppose it was simply easier to stay with Dan than to go through the stress of a divorce. Our marriage reminded me of a painting that I saw once. It was a piece called "Crystal Mask" by Erte, which shows a woman in fine clothing, holding a mask an inch away from her face. To me, I was that woman holding the mask, trying to appear as if everything was fine when it really wasn't.

After we'd been married for about twenty years, I became involved in politics and was known as a community leader. By this time, Dan and I were leading such separate lives that many people who knew both of us didn't even realize we were married. My political life kept me very busy, and Dan was busy in his life, or so I assumed. I suppose we could have gone on like this indefinitely—but then I had discovered something I couldn't ignore.

I discovered that Dan had become interested in watching pornography. He would rent videos, and I would catch him masturbating as he watched it. When I spoke to him about, it he said that it was "normal," because "all men do it." Perhaps surprisingly (because we were leading separate lives), we still had sex, but around this time I began to notice that our sex life was changing. It seemed like all Dan wanted to do was recreate the antics he saw on those videos. I began to suspect that maybe Dan was more involved with porn than just renting videos.

My defining moment came when I began to experience an unpleasant feeling and I thought I had a urinary tract infection. I went to the doctor who just scribbled a prescription for some pills he said I needed. He also informed me that I had contracted a STD and that my husband had already made his trip to the doctor's office and had been on an antibiotic treatment for two weeks. Dan never said a word to me and I know for certain that I did not give it to him, he gave it to me! While checking through his computer, I also discovered that he had been on twenty-two teen pornography sites in one day. I also found fifty-three porno films on his computer, and I saw that he had erased ninety-three films.

I was shocked and frightened. It suddenly became clear that Dan was not the man I thought he was. I had been oblivious to his shenanigans for a long time, but I realized then that it was time for me to wake up and regain my self-respect. I left him just before our thirtieth wedding anniversary and sent him a card that read: "This is our last anniversary. I married the wrong man."

The rebuilding process has been difficult, but I'm grateful for the support of my children. I am healing—slowly, but surely—and regaining my self-confidence.

While I was in the process of getting divorced, I put a new message on my answering machine: "I'm not able to take your call right now. As some of you know, I'm going through many changes in my life. If I don't call you back, you're one of the changes."

SANDY

~

Sandy has led a colorful life for most of her forty-one years. She's lived in several foreign countries, leaving home at age sixteen to strike out on her own. Now single again after a long-lasting but disappointing love affair, Sandy lives in San Diego, California, with her fifteen-year-old son. She is a talk-show host.

I was born in Israel to Guyanese parents. My dad, who was fascinated with the Jewish religion, had moved the family to Israel so he could convert from Christianity to Judaism. Our life was anything but calm; my dad became a religious fanatic, and that affected the entire family. We moved back to Guyana when I was nine—by this time there were six children in the family—and shortly after that, we had a terrible fire in our home. My mom rescued all six of her children, but my dad ran out of the house, only concerned with saving himself. I never forgot that my father never tried to save his family. I could see my mom's strength and his weakness; I could not understand why she stayed with him. He also cheated on her throughout their marriage, but although she sometimes threw him out, she always took him back. It was her pattern.

By the time I was a teenager, my dad denounced Judaism and became involved with David Koresh and the Branch Davidians. In retrospect, I think that my father was such a religious fanatic because he felt guilty being emotionally unavailable to the family.

I started turning to books to escape the turmoil in my family. I was so into fantasy that I thought my personal fairy tales would come true—I would meet a wonderful guy and live happily ever after. I left home at age sixteen because my father wouldn't let me date. I was able to get a visa, and I left for Brazil, where I worked for a wealthy German family as a housekeeper. The husband, Hans, often approached me in a flirtatious way. After a while, I could see he wasn't just flirting—he was hoping I would accept his advances, but I never gave in. I began to feel too uncomfortable with him, though, so I left that household. Sometime later, his wife died, and Hans pleaded with me to come back and work for him. I moved back in, and it wasn't long before we had a sexual relationship. In my mind, I was trading sex for his paying my expenses. Even so, I hated the fact I had to sleep with him. He was fifty-five, balding, and not particularly attractive. But I loved living the lavish and extravagant lifestyle he provided.

One night, when Hans and I were out dancing, I spotted a very attractive man. He had brown hair and beautiful hazel eyes, and he was very sexy. I quickly wrote my phone number on a piece of paper, and when I walked past him, I handed my number to him. He called me the next day.

I was now eighteen, and suddenly, I'd fallen head over heels for Peter, but the question remained: What was I going to do about Hans? So I lied to Peter, telling him that Hans was a friend of my father's and that I was staying with him while I went to school. And Hans was so in love with me, he would have been my slave. I, on the other hand, was in love with Peter, but I had lied to him about my circumstances. I felt in such a dilemma.

Brazil was such a beautiful place, and Rio de Janeiro, where I was living, had fabulous places to go for dinner and dancing. Peter, who was my age, would take me on wonderful dates. And we had the most incredible sex; it seemed that all we did was have sex. Then Peter would drive me back home to Hans. I desperately wanted to keep both lives—a life with Hans, with the rich façade, and a life with Peter, the man I loved.

I finally got the courage to tell Hans that I was in love with Peter. Not surprisingly, he asked me to move out. When I left his house, I went to America—in California—to work for my aunt. Conveniently, Peter's parents had a home in California, and he was coming to visit them there. Once Peter arrived in America, we were inseparable. His parents had a magnificent home on a hill overlooking the water. I stayed there with him for six months, and again it was like a fairy tale.

After the end of those six months, I went to Seattle, where my sister was living. But I was depressed. Peter had gone back to Brazil, where he returned to the university, but I was working in a factory and was afraid he'd find out. Peter often called me to ask when I was coming back to Brazil—after all, he didn't know I couldn't return to Hans' house. Finally, after several months, I saved enough money to return to Brazil. Fortunately, Peter had asked me to stay with him at his place, so I didn't have to explain about Hans. Peter and I rekindled our sexual relationship—it was just like it had been when we first met. But the fairy tale was about to come to an end: I got pregnant—and my defining moment was about to occur. *It happened when I told Peter about the baby. Rather than share in my joy, he immediately told me to have an abortion. I told him I couldn't do that to our child, and he told me, "You'll have the baby by yourself then."*

I was devastated and hurt. I thought he really loved me and wanted a life together. I returned to California to be close to my aunt. I was depressed, pregnant, and basically alone. Peter did not want to be bothered with a woman who was pregnant, especially because he also found out I wasn't wealthy, as he'd assumed all along.

It had finally become clear to me that he did not want me, but unlike in the past, I did not try to win him back. I had to break the pattern; I didn't want to be like my mom, who always decided to stay with my dad because she did not have the courage to leave him.

I'd like to say that I learned a good lesson from my relationship with Peter, but I still have relationships with men where I know I should leave, but I keep going back—back to relationships that are not good for me. Maybe that's because I am never "real" in my relationships; I always portray myself as something I am not. I admit that I live in my fantasy world and never let anyone see the real me. That's just the way I am.

PEARL

~

Intelligent and well-read, Pearl didn't always recognize her own worth. She had a difficult time with men and relationships because of a strong message she received throughout her life. Now, at age forty-nine, she has learned she can change the course of her own life, and she wants to be a motivating force for others. She volunteers at a domestic abuse shelter, where she helps young women to recognize their strengths and understand their self-worth. Pearl currently is not dating. She believes that it is important to see the seasons change for one year before she considers testing the dating waters again. She resides in Dallas, Texas.

---

*M*y parents never married. In fact, my father left my mother as soon as he discovered that she was pregnant. I am four minutes older than my twin brother. My mother wasn't able to care for us, so she sent us to live with her mother when we were three months old. My grandmother accepted this responsibility, but I know she always felt we were a burden. This made my childhood very unhappy. Although I was always clean, well fed and well dressed, I could tell my grandmother didn't want us there. I suppose she was busy enough with her own life.

My grandmother, who was only forty years old when my twin and I came to live with her, had experienced a lot of physical, emotional, and verbal abuse from the men she'd been involved with over the years. At the time my mother sent us to live with my grandmother, she had a live-in boyfriend, and he was just as abusive as the men in her past had been. As a result of her raising me in that type of environment, I saw my share of domestic violence, and as an adult, I believe that I played out the abuse cycle in all of my relationships.

When I was two years old, my grandmother's live-in boyfriend molested me. Through my many years in counseling, I have discovered that my grandmother more than likely knew that I had been molested, but she never acknowledged it. She was either afraid or unwilling to do anything about it. Instead of helping me to deal with it, I believe it became the source of her anger. She was always telling me that she hated me and that I would never amount to anything. I spent all of my childhood trying to get her to love me, but I was never able to gain her love. This attitude—from someone who should have loved me unconditionally—definitely set the stage for the types of relationships in which I later became involved.

I met George when I was still in high school. We started dating when I was fifteen and he was seventeen. I never particularly liked George, but I dated him in order to fit in at school. I also dated him because I didn't think that I could do much better. George and I were total opposites. I loved to read—it's how I spent most of my free time—but I'm not sure George even knew how to read. I wanted to go to college, but George wasn't too ambitious and never even thought about going to college.

Although my grandmother assured me that I wasn't smart enough or good enough to be accepted, I started filling out college applications. I soon proved her wrong—I not only was accepted to Spelman College (a prestigious college for African American women) but I also received a full scholarship. Toward the end of my senior year, however, my grandmother told me that I would not be able to go away to school, because she needed me around the house. She told me that I would be wasting my time at school anyway, because I would never amount to anything. I believed her, because I'd heard those words so many times before. So in the late summer of that year, as I watched my girlfriends pack their belongings and go off to college, I remained in town with George.

My relationship with George lasted for thirteen years—and they were the worst thirteen years of my life. Although he was never physically abusive toward me, he was emotionally abusive. He fathered three children—while he was dating me!—but I stayed with him because I felt it was better than being alone. George got me pregnant too, several times, but I had abortions. It got to the point that I was using abortion as a form of birth control while I was dating him.

My therapist later told me that I had so many abortions as a way of hurting my "inner child," who had been hurt through the molestation. At the time, though, I did not have the tools to get out of this relationship. Instead, I went into a deep depression. But my depression didn't prevent me from finally realizing George was not "the one." *My defining moment came when I discovered that George had actually married someone else—while he was still dating me.*

Even though I knew the relationship should have ended years ago, the fact that George was getting married to someone else while we were still dating was devastating to me. In fact, it was mind-boggling. I told everyone that if I ever saw George out on the street, I would kill him. And several weeks after his wedding, I came close to doing just that. I was driving around, actually trying to find him and I discovered him leaving his mother's house and approaching his car, and his new bride was sitting in the car waiting for him. When he walked into the street to get into the driver's side of the car, our eyes met I lost it and I floored my gas petal and I was aiming for him and he narrowly escaped my car by quickly jumping into his car, but he was unable to close his door, because I had knocked it clear off the hinges! After this incident, I spiraled into a deeper depression and ended up being hospitalized for three months. The hospitalization was a major transformation for me. Therapy was extremely helpful, and by the time I was released from the hospital, I was on the road to healing.

That is when I met Mike. I was twenty-nine when we met, and he was thirty. We dated for a while and eventually married, but the marriage didn't last long. Mike was a nice man, but he was extremely flirtatious. We would argue constantly about his flirtatious behavior, until one day, after four years of marriage, *I had my defining moment in the grocery store. I made up my mind that our relationship was over, and on that shopping trip—and from then on—I purchased groceries just for me: one steak, one potato, and just enough broccoli for one.* Soon after that, we were separated and then divorced.

But it was Bill who truly helped me to transform into the woman that I am today. Bill combined all the abuse that George and Mike had shown me over the years—at this point in my life, I still accepted it. Bill was a golf instructor, and we met at a golf outing when I was forty-five and he was fifty-eight. He was gentle and so kind when we first met, but as time went on, he became extremely possessive and was constantly checking up on me. My gut was telling me to run for the hills, but my heart said that I should at least get to know him.

Very early on, I realized that the littlest situation would quickly ignite him, and he had an explosive temper. He was always ready to push me down verbally as well as physically.

Sexually, Bill was extremely intense and passionate, but he would often ask me to do sexual things with him, and then after I fulfilled his request, he would call me a whore or slut. He would tell me that he loved me, but he often treated me unkindly. He would not only hit me, but he would let me know that he was stronger than I was, and so he could really hurt me if he wanted to. Logically, I knew I had to get out of this relationship, but I didn't have the heart to act.

And then I had my defining moment: We had gone to the coffee shop and were sitting in the car, talking, as we waited for the coffee to cool.

We got into an argument, and before I knew what was happening, Bill got out of the car, came around to my side and opened my door, and threw his coffee in my face! That was when I knew for sure that I was doing the right thing in breaking up with him. I knew I had finally had enough, and I couldn't allow him to continue to abuse me any longer.

Bill did not go easily; he continued to hound me and beg me to get back together with him. But somehow, I was able to remain strong. And I can see now that my own strength helped me to get out from bad relationships. In the past, I refused to trust my instincts, and I believed that I failed to do so because of all of the years of hearing that I wasn't "good enough." Now I know better. I know for sure that if a man is acting crazy on the onset of a relationship, when he should be trying to impress you, the crazy behavior is only going to intensify as the relationship progresses.

CLARISSA

~

Clarissa never wanted to get married, not even when she knew she wanted to have children. She preferred to follow the example of those insects that bite the head off their mate after copulation—she just wanted a "specimen" to impregnate her. And then she met the man who would change her mind. Now forty-eight years old and separated from her husband, she's working to rebuild her life. Clarissa lives with her four children in Baltimore, Maryland. She's a housewife.

When I met Lenny, I had just turned twenty and he was almost twenty-three. I'm not sure what attracted me to him. Although we met in the '80s, he was still sporting a '70s haircut, and he was a heavy-set guy with a huge belly; he was the kind of guy I normally was not attracted to.

I knew his dad before I met Lenny, because his dad was my boss. He always sounded so proud of his boys, but I later found out that he never spent any time with his kids. Lenny's father also was abusive to his mother. He had a really explosive temper—he hit first and asked questions later.

When I started going out with Lenny, I hoped that he would not repeat his dad's pattern. But I didn't really worry about it; he seemed like such a nice guy. I introduced him to my world of art galleries and dance performances. He was receptive, but it was different for him. He usually just liked to hang out with his friends and drink beer.

My dad thought my dating Lenny was the biggest mistake of my life. Dad saw Lenny as selfish, and he felt when the chips were down, Lenny would put himself first.

After we'd been dating for two and a half years, Lenny proposed to me. We had talked a lot about getting engaged. In fact, Lenny had spoken to my brother about proposing, although he wasn't as traditional as asking my dad for my hand in marriage. Maybe he knew my dad wouldn't give us his blessing.

Lenny and I got married, with about 125 guests at the wedding. I was so excited when I walked down the aisle—this was my dream. We honeymooned in England and had a wonderful time. Shortly after we returned, I learned that my mom was quite ill. She and my dad had split up when I was seven, so she was all by herself out in North Dakota. I went out there to be with her, and I stayed there with her for two months, until she died. Lenny was supportive during this time; it was really hard for me when my mom died.

Within the next several years I had three pregnancies that did not go to term. Two were early miscarriages and one pregnancy was terminated in the fourth month because of abnormalities. During these times, Lenny also was supportive.

When I finally got pregnant again, I was able to carry the baby to term and delivered a healthy baby girl. Initially, Lenny was helpful, but as time went on he began to spend more time out of the house. In the next five years we had two more kids, and Lenny became more and more distant. I knew he was working hard and becoming more financially successful, but I felt isolated. I was home with the kids while he was out in the world, taking care of his business. Also, Lenny began to talk to me as if I were a child. He was insulting, too—he called me a mental and physical marshmallow.

Then I became pregnant with our fourth child. I was mortified; I didn't want to have another child. I considered terminating the pregnancy, but Lenny begged me to reconsider. He said if I would have the baby, he would provide a nanny for me. I agreed, and Lenny followed through on his promise and hired his nephew, Matt, as a live-in nanny. Matt was great with the kids, and he really became part of our family. Matt would often invite his friend Dawn over to the house, and she also became like a family member—she even called us Aunt Clarissa and Uncle Lenny. I noticed that Lenny was more fun-loving when Dawn visited, but I figured that was because she was young and he was trying to keep up with her and Matt.

My defining moment came when I caught Lenny with Dawn in an embrace that said she was much more to Lenny than a "family member"—he was having an affair with her.

I couldn't believe that this girl, who was treated like one of our family, had betrayed me with my husband. It also upset me that my kids all adored her—she's like a big kid to them—and it seems so unfair to me that she stole my husband and my children. In fact, when she first started visiting our house, she once said to me, "You have the American Dream—a beautiful house, nice cars, wonderful kids, and a nice husband. I hope I get to have what you have." I didn't know she meant that literally. Although I threw Lenny out when I caught him with Dawn, I'm in no hurry to grant him a divorce so he can marry her.

Currently, I am trying to get my life back together. I am actively involved in my children's lives, and I'm contemplating going back to school to finish my degree. I also have a new boyfriend, who respects me and treats me as an equal. But more importantly, I am regaining my sense of self-worth, and that feels so good.

DONNA

~

Fifty-five-year-old Donna is the first to admit that she always felt that she needed to be with a man, but two failed relationships did much damage to her self-esteem. Now, she is working on being more being self-reliant. Donna, who works in an art gallery, has two grown children and lives in Evansville, Indiana.

---

*F*rom the time I was ten years old, I realized that my parents had an unusual relationship. Every spring, my dad would get "spring fever"—he would begin a relationship with a new woman. It wasn't that he didn't love my mom, but he always had to have a different woman. I know that my mom was devastated and hurt by his antics, but she continued to put up with his affairs because of the security of being taken care of.

Growing up, all I knew was that I didn't want to have a marriage like my parents had. I always thought that if I did everything by the book, my love life would turn out okay. I always hoped to find someone who would love me and consider me his equal and that our relationship would be exclusive. I did not want to emulate my mother, staying with a man who cheated on me just for security.

But that's just what I ended up doing. I was married for twenty-two years to my first husband, and he went to strip clubs and had girlfriends almost the entire time. And like my mother, I put up with it. We had two children together, but that never stopped his outside "activities." We only divorced because my husband decided that *he* was tired of *me*.

After my divorce I became involved with a support group for divorced parents, and that is when I met Sam. He looked like a professor, with his glasses and tweed jacket. He was eight years my senior, but he seemed like a nice guy, so I agreed to go out on a date with him—we went to the movies. As the weeks went on and we went on more dates, I realized that he only wanted to go to the movies. I enjoyed movies, but I also liked to do other things, like going to concerts, eat in restaurants, and go dancing.

The only time he would take me to dances was when our support group would organize one. When we went to these dances, though, Sam would introduce me to others as his "friend"; he didn't want anyone to know we were dating. Even worse, he would dance with his former girlfriends who were there. Sam's philosophy was that he had to stay friends with his previous girlfriends. At times when we would go places, there were four or five ex-girlfriends there, and he thought it was perfectly normal to spend time with them. This kind of behavior started to remind me of my dad's spring fever, and I hated it!

Finally, I had had enough; we stopped seeing each other for about six months. During that time, Sam started seeing another woman—Margie. Eventually, Sam asked me to take him back, and I agreed. But after we got back together, Margie confronted me at a party and told me that she had been seeing Sam for the entire time we were together—including the first two years of our relationship. I was dumbfounded. I couldn't believe he had been so deceitful.

When I confronted him about what Margie had said, he finally admitted that they had seen each other in the past, but he assured me that it was over. And again he said that he didn't see anything wrong with remaining friends. Eventually, he sweet talked me, and I forgave him. He still would never tell any of his female friends that he and I were dating.

My defining moment occurred one Christmas. My now-adult children were visiting and we all were waiting for Sam so we could have dinner. He called to tell me that an "old friend" had stopped by and he wanted to visit with her. Could I change the time of our dinner?

That was the last straw. I told him to forget about dinner and to get out of my life. I had spent six years with a man who thrived on the attention of other women, and I was tired of it. I deserved better than this.

I'm wiser now, and I've finally come to realize that it's better to be alone than to be in an awful relationship. I'm now happily on my own. I'm financially stable and pursuing my own passion of helping others who are going through divorce. I've also made the conscious decision to be as successful as I can be and not be a victim. I'm only relying on myself to be happy.

BRIDGETTE

~

Bridgette fell for the shining smile and smooth conversation of a fellow student, but even when she later found out that appearances could be deceiving—and she was being played for a fool—she couldn't bring herself to leave him. Now forty-eight years old, Bridgette says that it took her many years to accept her own role in the "mess" that was her first marriage. Ultimately, however, she was able to move on with her life. Today, Bridgette is happily remarried. She works for Port Authority and lives in Trenton, New Jersey.

I was raised in a very religious household. My parents were very loving toward one another and to me and my brother and foster sisters. My father was extremely hard working and my mother had a very entrepreneurial spirit—she sold makeup door to door. Because I grew up in a nice home with hard-working, drug-free parents, I always expected that once I got married, my life would be pretty similar to my parents' way of living.

There was a couple who lived up the block from me when I was a child, and I always wanted to emulate them too. I spent a lot of time dreaming and wishing that one day I would meet someone, get married, and be just like them. Little did I know that other things were in store for me.

The first time I saw Phil was when we both were watching a football game at school. I was fifteen years old at the time, and Phil was seventeen. Our eyes immediately met across the crowd, and he later came over to me and introduced himself. He asked me for my phone number, and at first, I wouldn't give it to him. But I did think he was cute, and he had one of the biggest and whitest smiles that I had ever seen. I don't remember how long it took, but I eventually gave in and gave him my telephone number. He began calling me and coming by my house. My mother was always so kind-hearted, and she never had anything bad to say about anyone, so she immediately loved him. But my father could see things crystal clear; he didn't like Phil at all.

Right from the beginning, I realized that Phil and I had not been raised the same way. His mother was a single parent to twelve kids by five different fathers. Phil and his eleven brothers and sisters were often left alone to raise themselves. Phil and I started spending more time over at his house, because we could "fool around" easier—his mother was hardly ever home. We were not sexually intimate at this time, because I was fifteen and still a virgin. Phil wanted to have sex, but I wanted to wait—at least for a little while. As it turned out, Phil decided not to wait for me. I found out that there was another girl waiting upstairs in one of the rooms in Phil's big house. Since I wasn't willing to put out, he went upstairs to get the other girl and then told me that I was leaving and she was staying.

I don't know why that tactic worked on me, but I was not going to lose Phil, so I decided that it was time for me to lose my virginity. By the time I was sixteen and he was eighteen, Phil and I were having sex on a regular basis. Sex wasn't the only thing that Phil and I did for entertainment; he also introduced me to smoking pot and smoking cigarettes. I knew that I wasn't the only girl that Phil was sleeping with—at least, that's what the rumors were. But the rumors did have some basis in fact—throughout our relationship, other girls would just walk up to me and inform me that they were sleeping with Phil. He would deny this, of course, and this became a pattern in our relationship.

Then once I turned seventeen, I decided it was time to talk about marriage. Phil said that he was ready to settle down and that he wanted to marry me. But I kept hearing about rumors about Phil's involvement with other girls—and one girl in particular. Eventually, Phil was no longer able to deny the rumors, because that girl—Rachel—got pregnant. I was devastated, and I never told anyone, including my friends or family, that Rachel was pregnant with Phil's baby. Phil insisted that he didn't want to marry Rachel; he wanted to marry me.

Rachel gave birth to her baby, but Phil never involved himself with the child. That should have been a red flag, but I honestly was just glad that I didn't have to "share" him with another woman and her child. But as our relationship continued, the rumors about Phil and other women continued. One day I decided to go over to his house to surprise him. Well, the surprise was on me. I found him with another girl—and she was wearing my lingerie that I kept there! But did I break up with Phil? Of course not.

By the age of nineteen, any choice of leaving Phil, as far as I was concerned, was taken away from me: I was pregnant. I didn't know what to do, but Phil was insistent that we get married and keep the baby. I was scared because I knew that he already had one child that he did not take care of. But I wondered if marriage was the answer to making Phil a faithful partner.

I was four months pregnant on our wedding day, and Phil was a nervous wreck. He came close to fainting several times. When I look back on our wedding day, I specifically remember thinking that because we went through a wedding ceremony, Phil's infidelity would stop. Instead, it intensified. He had other women throughout our marriage, even when I was pregnant and even when we had a new baby. He seemed almost uncontrollable. By the time our daughter was born—we'd been married about three years at this time—I realized that Phil had another favorite activity: He was doing cocaine. This, however, was just a prologue to his shooting up heroin. During this time, Phil began a revolving cycle of being in and out of jail for drug possession. It was becoming increasingly difficult for him to get or maintain a job because of his criminal record. And that is when he resorted to robbery as a way of making an income.

I realized that I couldn't live like this any longer. I was tired of dragging our kids off to prison to see him. When Phil called from jail—again—to tell me he'd been arrested for his involvement in another robbery, I told him it was the end of our marriage.

For five years, the kids and I went on with our lives, and it felt good. There were no lies or deception going on. A huge load had been lifted from me. But by the time those five years were up and Phil was paroled, he came home—and my heart and my body couldn't refuse him.

Of course, life with Phil went right back to where it had been. Phil couldn't find a job, and I knew that he had women at the house while I was at work all day.

And then 9/11 happened. My youngest foster sister worked in one of the towers, and my family was distraught, assuming that she had perished in the incident. I was also tortured by the fact that she and I hadn't spoken much recently—she basically broke off communication with me shortly after I started dating Phil. I wished that I'd taken a more active role in staying in touch with her.

Then, very late that evening she called to let me know she was all right. I was so relieved! We were both crying and saying how much we loved each other. After a while, she apologized for not speaking to me over the years. I tried to tell her it was okay, but she seemed determined to give me a reason why she'd backed away from me.

And that was my defining moment. I knew in that instant, without a doubt, that Phil wasn't and never would be "the one," because my sister told me that while Phil and I were dating, and she was a young teenager, Phil was forcing her to have sex with him.

She'd been too afraid to tell me at the time, because she knew how much I loved him. But she realized that she'd come close to dying in that tower, and she didn't want to hold things in anymore. And she didn't want Phil to make a fool of me any longer.

Phil, of course, denied what my sister had told me. But I knew the truth, and I knew for sure that I had to get rid of him. I realized that by being with Phil, I would never advance. He was unreliable and was a cheat, drug abuser, and liar. I didn't need him; he was dead wood. So after twenty years of marriage, I finally divorced him. And it felt good.

Now, I am married to a man who is similar to my dad. He is soft-spoken, quiet, and hard-working. His main goal in life is to take care of me and our family—he is a family man in every sense of the word. I think that was what I was yearning for all along.

GWEN

~

Gwen wanted to emulate her parents' wonderful relationship, but none of the men she dated seemed like husband material—until she met Stan. With his powerful presence, he seemed like the man of her dreams. Although their relationship eventually became a nightmare, Gwen walked away with her self-respect intact. Now fifty-eight years old, Gwen is contentedly single and living in Los Angeles, where she works in the human resources department of a major department store.

---

*I*f I could have found a fabulous man like my dad, I would have been a happy woman. My parents always had an excellent relationship. They were in love, always holding hands until the day my dad died. They were absolutely made for each other and were married for fifty-three years. They showed my younger sister and me the true meaning of love and marriage.

I had boyfriends in college, but I wasn't serious about any of them. Maybe I was too focused on my studies, or maybe they just seemed immature. Once I graduated college and started working, I dated occasionally, but again, no man ever meant enough to me to establish a long-term relationship. Maybe I was searching too hard for a guy like my dad, and I just never found him.

I first met Stan when I was forty-three and he was fifty. After years of trying to find "the one" for me by chance, I decided to respond to a personal ad in the newspaper. Stan and I spoke on the phone a couple of times—I learned he was a widower with two grown children—and then decided to meet for dinner. When I walked into the restaurant and saw him, I was dumbstruck. There was just something about him that drew me to him like a magnet. He was big, blond, and very attractive; he simply oozed sensuality. We talked so much that evening that neither of us ate much dinner, so we made a date for another night—and soon we were dating exclusively.

Stan had a remarkable, commanding presence. He was a high-ranking official with the Los Angeles Fire Department, and he had a look of authority. Even though I was incredibly attracted to him, Stan came from a world quite alien to me—he was a blue-collar worker who came from a working-class background, and he hadn't gone to college. His dad died when he was a teenager, and he had had to go to work to support the family. He was an outdoorsman and was into hunting and fishing. But it was his strong camaraderie with his "brothers" in the fire department that I found most fascinating—they truly shared a special bond, and I was impressed by that kind of loyalty.

Stan was very outspoken and had very definite opinions on things. There was nothing delicate, nothing sensitive, nothing polished about the man, and he was completely self-educated. He was rather unrefined, but he could be amazingly perceptive and insightful. I was mesmerized by the many facets of his personality.

The first time I met Stan's family was at a wedding for his late wife's niece—he had remained close to his in-laws. Now I was also to meet his daughters. I was extremely nervous, but Stan assured me they would accept me because they didn't want him to be alone for the rest of his life. I needn't have worried; the guests at the wedding (Stan's daughters included) were far more interested in the wedding revelry. I had never been to a wedding where a drunken brawl broke out and pitchers of beer were thrown at people. At one point I asked Stan if this type of behavior was normal. He shrugged amiably and said that this was his "world." Well, in my world, there would have been a three-piece band playing soft music as the wedding guests sipped champagne. This was really different for me—but I was attracted by his bad-boy persona.

At the beginning of our relationship, Stan was so tender and kind to me, but as time went on, I guess we started to take each other for granted. The little romantic gestures became less frequent, and Stan no longer was as supportive as he could have been. This became especially apparent to me when my darling father had a heart attack and died. I was devastated, of course, but I knew I could rely on Stan's strength to support me during the funeral.

Then Stan decided he could not take the day off to attend the funeral. At this point we had been dating exclusively for five months, and I'd come to rely on him. I was furious that he would not take the day off. I felt he should have been there for me. Later, he came to my apartment, just as he usually did after work. He knew that I was upset, but he was very detached from his emotions.

By this time, I had learned that Stan was a controlled alcoholic. He could consume an enormous quantity of alcohol on any given night. Usually, he was able to handle his liquor, but his episodes of getting staggering drunk were happening more and more frequently. Although I didn't like it, I didn't want to let him go because I was so in love with him.

My defining moment was startlingly simple: Over breakfast one morning, Stan said, "I know this is very shallow of me, but I don't find you attractive anymore. I'm going to start dating other women."

Of course, what he really meant was that he already was dating other women. I went absolutely berserk—screaming, crying, throwing clothes around the room. I have never felt so out of control—or so helpless. I could have tried to persuade him to change his mind, but I at least was able to keep my self-respect: I told Stan that our relationship was officially over.

From this experience I learned men are more trouble than they're worth. Since breaking up with Stan, I've had no urge to be involved with anybody else again. I'm happier and more at peace than ever before.

JOAN

~

Joan knows quite a bit about self-sacrifice—she stayed in an intolerable marriage for five years in order to be a full-time mom to her daughter. Now a lively sixty-year-old, whose youthful appearance belies her age, Joan enjoys her life in Malibu, California, where she has been happily single for the past twenty-four years. Joan is the proud mother of an Academy Award-winning actress. She is an owner of an antique shop.

I grew up in a tiny, one-bedroom apartment that was shared by my parents, my grandmother, and me. My grandmother and I slept in the bedroom (her bed was behind a curtain in the room), and my parents slept on a fold-out couch in the living room. This lack of privacy put an awful strain on my parents' marriage. Because my parents had a lack of intimacy in their marriage, my father had girlfriends most of the time—my mother was fully aware of this. She was a very angry woman, and I was the one who bore the brunt of her anger.

As a child, I was not allowed to verbally express myself, and so I had a lot of pent-up feelings. I decided very earlier on that if I had a daughter, I would encourage her to talk to me about anything. I thought that if I got married, it should be to somebody that I could talk to, somebody who would listen to me. I was just looking for someone to be my friend.

I was twenty-two before I had my first serious boyfriends. The first one decided that he was in love with someone else shortly after we started dating, and the second one finally admitted to himself that he was gay after we'd been dating about a year.

So at twenty-five years old and having graduated from college, I returned to my parents' tiny apartment. Today, twenty-five doesn't seem so old to not be married, but this was back in the 1970s, and I was on the verge of becoming an old maid.

Then that's when I met Walter.

I was teaching at the time, and one of my colleagues at school said that she wanted to introduce her brother to me, so we arranged to meet at a small party at her house. As soon as I walked into the room and saw Walter, I thought that he was much too old for me. Walter was only thirty-one, but he had an older demeanor and just seemed like an old man. He wasn't particularly good-looking either.

I suppose that my self-esteem was at a low point when I met Walter because although I was not attracted to him, I decided to give him my phone number. I told myself that I should be attracted to him because he had admirable qualities—he had a good job (he was a lawyer); he came from a really nice family; he was very respectful; he had his own apartment and his own car. Probably most importantly, because he quickly showed interest in me, I kept thinking that he would never leave me, which made me feel safe. I also thought that a relationship with Walter was a good idea because he was able to offer the one thing I had been looking for, ever since I was young: Walter was able to communicate with me and be my friend.

We had only four dates before Walter wanted me to meet his parents, and shortly after that, Walter asked me to move in with him. I agreed, because I was certain that it would be just a matter of time before he asked me to marry him—he seemed to be leading up to that.

I thought Walter would be a good catch. I knew that he was a very smart man, and I became impressed by his intelligence. He also was very funny, and at that point in my life, I had really needed to laugh. He wasn't terribly romantic—I'd always wanted lots of romance—but even so, I had grown to love Walter. The one problem in our relationship was the sex—he wasn't very good at it. Throughout our relationship, sex was a difficult topic, because after a while, I didn't want to have it with him—he just couldn't satisfy me, and I didn't like his style. There was never any warning—no transition to sex. We would go from talking about something, like which peanut butter to buy, and he would jump right into a quick foreplay, and then, before I knew it, we were in the actual act. But in spite of there being no romance and a terrible sex life, once he approached the subject of marriage, I was ready to jump in.

The early years of our marriage were challenging because of the lack of sex in our marriage. He kept insisting that I was frigid, and he'd tell me that I wasn't being a good wife and wasn't paying any attention to him. Eventually, I started to believe him, and my self-esteem hit rock bottom. I felt as though I was withering away.

We must have had some sex, though, because three years into our marriage, I discovered that I was pregnant. I'll never forget his reaction to the news—he seemed catatonic, as if he were a statue. His face showed no expression at all. That sums up the way he acted throughout most of my pregnancy—he acted as if it didn't exist. Of course I was scared of his reaction, because the baby wasn't even here yet, and he was already ignoring it. I was most furious because he was so unresponsive about my pregnancy.

Then, for no discernable reason about three weeks before my due date, Walter agreed to accompany me to Lamaze class. I do have to say that once he made the commitment to go to the classes, he became involved—but maybe that wasn't such a sacrifice: three short weeks out of nine months.

What I really resented was that after the baby was born—my beautiful baby girl—Walter would tell people the story of her birth with such gusto, as if he were really an involved father. It took every ounce of strength for me not to tell people how awful he'd been through most of my pregnancy. Really, I was just so angry at him from day one of my pregnancy that I almost felt as if he wasn't entitled to be happy about it at any point. But I just let go of that feeling. I didn't deal with a lot of things back then.

Our baby, though healthy and perfect, was a bit jaundiced as a newborn. It's a common condition, but the doctor wanted to keep her in the hospital for another couple of days so she could be placed under special lights as a treatment. He said that I could go home and come to visit her during the day.

I refused to leave my baby in the hospital, so I told Walter that I would stay with her until she could come home. But Walter wanted to take me home right then—he was concerned about the additional cost we'd incur if I stayed in the hospital for two more days. He gave no thought to my feelings about it.

I did win that argument—I just refused to leave—but by this point, I was beginning to get angry with Walter more often, because I no longer felt that he was listening to me when I talked to him.

My defining moment came on the day the baby and I came home from the hospital. I walked into the apartment, carrying the baby in my arms, and when I turned to speak to Walter, he was already halfway down the hall, on his way back to work.

I stood there in shock. He'd acted as if there was nothing out of the ordinary about the fact we'd just brought our first baby home from the hospital, but worse than that, he wasn't even aware of the fact that I might need him to be there with me on that first day.

That single act seemed to define where I was in our marriage—alone. I broke away from Walter, emotionally, at that moment. I knew that I was finished with him.

Unfortunately, I ended up staying in that miserable marriage until my daughter's fifth birthday. I didn't want to send her to daycare; I wanted to be there for my daughter every day, which I wouldn't have been able to do if I was working. So I stayed with Walter for those five years so I could be a stay-at-home mom. Our marriage, however, was a sham. I didn't want Walter to touch me sexually; I didn't even want to be near him. I think we both were miserable in our marriage.

When my daughter was old enough for kindergarten, I knew I would be able to return to work—and that's when I told Walter that I could not take another second of being married to him. The hardest part was breaking the news to my daughter. It was truly one of the most painful days in my life. Still, I know it was the right decision. I am proud of the fact that I was able to think things out logically and was able to stay home with my daughter and make her my priority.

I have never once had any regrets about divorcing Walter. Right before we signed our divorce papers, Walter asked me if I expected to find someone who was "better" than he was. I told him that I wasn't looking for someone better; I wasn't looking for anyone. I simply wanted to get my life back on track. And I have. In fact, I find this whole man-woman relationship really remarkable. It's remarkable to me that there are actually people who can stay together for any length of time. It's now a difficult notion for me to comprehend.

KAREN

~

As a "flower child" in the 1960s, Karen led a free-spirited existence with her husband—hitchhiking across Europe and getting
involved in the drug scene. She admits that he seemed to have mesmerized her into accepting a life that was quite unlike the one she'd
originally pictured for herself. Now divorced—and remaining single
by choice—fifty-nine-year-old Karen is living life on her own terms.
She is a yoga instructor who resides in Woodstock, New York.

When I was growing up, I always dreamed that I'd find a man
who would be a good provider, someone who could take care
of me and take me places. I suppose I saw the hard life that my parents had—my dad was a truck driver and Mom was a stay-at-home
mother, so we didn't have a lot of money—and I wanted more out
of my own life.

It might seem funny, then, that I was attracted to Rob. If someone
had placed an ad that read "Wanted: man who has no job and is
totally anti-social," Rob would have been perfect for it. He was
twenty-five when I met him (I was twenty), and he looked very
rebellious. He had long blond hair, and his appearance was a cross
between Jim Morrison and Kris Kristofferson—two very hot singers
back in the '60s. He seemed unconventional and mysterious, and I
was immediately attracted to him. We met in art school. I noticed
Rob because he was a brilliant painter. I was really impressed with
his work.

We went for coffee and exchanged phone numbers. We hadn't been dating very long when Rob said we should go to Europe. It seemed so spontaneous and fun! I just wanted to escape, so I agreed to go with him. I turned into a flower child—I stopped shaving my legs and didn't even wear a bra. I loved being non-traditional. It felt like Rob was taking me on the magical mystery tour; we hitchhiked our way through Europe, often living in cheap houses for seven dollars a month. He was always so mysterious and he got even more mysterious after a while. And I just followed right along. I cut off all my ties with my family so that I could be with him. Looking back now, I realize I gave up my entire identity to be with him. I really didn't know what the hell I was doing.

When we came back to the United States, we got a minibus and put up curtains on the windows, like in *The Partridge Family*. We went to Woodstock, where we had a wild time. I was loving life as a free spirit. About a year and a half later, Rob and I eloped. We were married by a Justice of the Peace and then went out for dinner; that was the end of our wedding day.

There were so many red flags that indicated our relationship was doomed, but being young and foolish, I chose to ignore them. Rob wasn't working. He had no ambition, other than to become the next Picasso. Yet he felt I should support him in his dreams. Somehow, I fell into that role.

He was taking drugs while we were in Europe and continued to do so when we got home. Lots of people were smoking pot and taking LSD in those days. I often joined him, just because my frame of mind was that I would go along with whatever he did. I really didn't have an idea or opinion on my own; I was just mesmerized by him. Logically, I knew that Rob was such an obnoxious person, and I don't know why that appealed to me, but it did. He was able to outwit and intimidate people. In a way, he was like Charles Manson. He had a certain power to mesmerize people so that they would just follow him. And he exuded a certain kind of energy that attracted people to him; they just sort of gathered around him.

When I would confront Rob about his lack of motivation to find real work or do anything other than paint, he would fly off into a rage. He would throw such tantrums. He felt he would eventually make money with his paintings. He never realized that he brought nothing to the table in terms of money; all he offered me was a lot of grief and sorrow. He was a bad seed, and he infected me and permeated my soul to the point that I got physically sick—I developed problems with my lower back and my neck.

Our life went on like this for years. During this time, Rob was in and out of the hospital for psychological problems and for abusing the prescription drugs the doctors gave him. He was drinking a lot, too, which made living with him very difficult. Eventually, he had to go to detox and then was admitted to a psychiatric hospital,

It was during his stay in the hospital that I had my defining moment. Rob would call me and threaten me over the phone, telling me how he would hurt me when he got out. I knew he wasn't well, but even so, those phone calls really finished it for me. In fact, I had been advised earlier by the hospital staff that I should tell Rob that our relationship was over, but I hadn't been able to muster up the courage. After his threatening phone calls, though, I knew I'd had enough. I could no longer deal with him. I had witnessed Rob's becoming progressively more unstable. Now, I had to let go of the situation. This guy was tearing me apart, and I had to do something for myself.

I got an order of protection for when—or if—he got out of the hospital. And then I filed for divorce. Rob was released after about a month, but I never saw him again. Less than a year later, he died. His cousin called me to say Rob had been found in the Hudson River. The specifics of how he died were unknown.

It's probably unkind, but when I learned that Rob was dead, I felt no sadness; I was relieved that I would never have to run into him on the street. I would never have to be fearful that he would find me. Part of me thanked God for the permanent solution.

Now my life is my own. I'm happily single and unattached. I'm learning about peace and doing wonderful things for myself, like meditation and spending time with friends. I've evolved so much since my relationship with Rob. I feel like I've come out a winner in spite of all my difficulties. I have a lot of zest for life ... and I live for today.

AMY

⁓

Thirty-eight-year old Amy recognizes the value of knowing when to cut her losses. She ended both of her long-term relationships when it was clear to her that she was traveling down a dead-end street. Currently single, Amy resides in Martha's Vineyard, Massachusetts, where she is an Obstetrician and Gynecologist.

I always expected to have a traditional marriage. Unlike my parents—both of whom had affairs during their marriage—I would not tolerate cheating from my husband. I was determined that my marriage would not only be perfect, but it also would last forever.

Two months after I graduated from college, however, I married a man who was seventeen years my senior. I had become depressed after a favorite uncle died, and I suppose I was looking for someone to take care of me. I made the mistake of marrying someone I didn't really know and who was much too old for me, just because I was at a low point in my life. But while I was looking for someone to take care of me, my husband was looking for a traditional "wife"—someone who would take care of him. Once I realized that, I quickly snapped out of the fog. I came to terms with myself and realized that I didn't really want to be a wife. Even though I was initially committed to this marriage, I eventually tired of the situation, and I divorced him.

I decided to focus most of my attention on my career. I was still looking for love, but I didn't really think I would find it. And then, when I was thirty-five, I met Ilya.

Ilya was one of the smartest men that I had ever met, and I was instantly attracted to his greatness. He was a Russian mathematician at MIT and was studying for his post-doctoral degree there. We talked for hours and hours at this party, mostly about abstract ideas. Our conversation didn't take on a personal tone until he asked me for my phone number. He called me the next day—and on several more days after that—and we never ran out of things to talk about. I thought he was endlessly fascinating. We soon discovered that we lived just three blocks away from each other, and we found it funny that both of us had lived in our apartments for three years, but we had never bumped into one another.

There was a lot of physical attraction between us that was pretty intense, and we quickly developed a relationship. We were together constantly, even spending the night at each other's apartment. We also had a lot of soul-searching sessions together; our relationship was very spiritual. We seemed destined to be together.

The longer I was with Ilya, however, the easier it was for me to recognize that he had a fear of commitment. He also was unable to react to other people's emotions. If I ever got upset about anything, rather than simply comforting me, he would quickly try to resolve whatever situation was bothering me. He was incapable of showing sympathy or compassion. I spent many hours trying to explain to him that not all problems can be quickly solved, like a math problem.

We also eventually developed issues in the bedroom. Although we began the relationship with intense physical passion, by the time we'd been together for a few months, I could see a problem—I always needed more intimacy, but Ilya would disconnect immediately, simply rolling over after sex, without any emotions or expressive thoughts about the act that had just taken place.

We did have fun together, of course. We traveled a lot while we were dating. We went to Italy several times, as well as to other parts of Europe. We also went to Hawaii, Jamaica, and Mexico. Ilya really seemed to be able to relax when we vacationed together, and it was always enjoyable for both of us.

Still, his emotionless personality was becoming increasingly hard to accept. After dating him for over two years, I had grown tired of his callous ways, especially as it seemed clear he would never make a firm commitment to me. In fact, he seemed intent on sabotaging our relationship. First, he told me that he needed space, which I didn't understand—I was hardly the clingy type of woman. Next, he started talking on the phone to an ex-girlfriend. I didn't think he was cheating on me, nor do I think he was ever interested in doing so, but he definitely was into creating triangles.

And then there was the ongoing issue with his lack of emotion. One day I was crying about something, and his only reaction was to ask how he could fix the problem. It wasn't until I told him that I just needed a hug that he even recognized what needed to be "fixed" at that moment was me. I spent way too much time directing him, emotionally. He usually recognized when something was bothering me, but he never knew what to do about it.

My defining moment came three years into our relationship, when I caught Ilya on the telephone with his ex-girlfriend. He tried to tell me, as he always did, that it was a platonic conversation, but he also admitted that he had been talking to her for several months without my knowing it, because he was trying to help her with her emotional problems.

I was stunned. I honestly don't know how much of what he said was true; it was just as likely that he was making it up as a way to sabotage our relationship, because he was fearful of commitment. All I do know is that I realized then that I could not trust him. And I could not be in a relationship with someone I couldn't trust.

Did I waste three years of my life in that relationship? Yeah, I probably did, but I was smart enough to cut my losses and walk away.

It's funny to know that when my friends and family first met Ilva, they all told me how much they liked him and how perfect he was, but when I announced that we were no longer together, almost everyone admitted to me that throughout the entire time of us dating, they hated him and couldn't wait for him to fall into a big black hole. Collectively, they despised him because they couldn't stand the fact that he was such an emotional waste-land.

For now, I am content with focusing on my career. I date occasionally but nothing too serious, and for me, life is good.

CYNTHIA

~

Love, as thirty-nine-year-old Cynthia discovered, is sometimes not enough. When she entered into a relationship with the man she thought was "the one," all she knew was that she loved him. Now happily single again, she has come to realize that although he professed love for her, too, she deserved more than he was able to give.

Cynthia lives in Myrtle Beach, South Carolina, where she is a pharmacist. She is in no hurry to become involved in a relationship again.

---

*M*y parents are celebrating their fiftieth wedding anniversary, but their marriage has been anything but blissful. They have lived almost separate lives. Mom stayed home with the kids, and Dad went off and did his own thing. They really didn't seem to support each other.

Maybe that's why I always wished that I would marry a man who was supportive and respectful of whatever I wanted to do. I envisioned an equal partnership—we would be on equal footing in our careers and in our lives. It seemed a reasonable wish.

When I met Joel, I was impressed by his smile, which lit up the room. He was the brother of a friend I'd met in pharmacy school, and although I didn't like "fix-ups," I was won over by his wonderful smile and his warm personality. We started dating after that first blind date, and six months later, we moved in together.

Joel was my first long-term relationship. In the past I'd had a fear of commitment, but I really felt a close connection to Joel. He was romantic and considerate. I remember when we first moved in together, we had no furniture. He put together a picnic on the floor in the bedroom, with chicken and champagne, and we toasted to our new apartment. I enjoyed spending time alone with him, but as the weeks went on, I learned that was all he wanted to do.

He didn't want to go out with other people; he just wanted to be with me. He seemed uncomfortable around anyone else. I had thought that he seemed shy when we first met, but I figured he was just nervous to be on a blind date. The few times I coaxed him out with my friends, he hardly spoke the entire evening.

It soon became apparent to me that Joel was drinking excessively. I suppose it was a way for him to cope, but when he drank he would become so belligerent and nasty. When I confronted him when he was sober about this behavior, he would be embarrassed and promise to quit drinking. That, however, would never last for long.

I should have noticed the red flags, but I didn't. I kept telling myself that he loved me and would change, but he never did. And as years went by, I felt stuck in the situation because we were living together and everyone expected us to get married.

Joel kept getting more and more reclusive. He did not want to go out socially at all. Social situations were very painful for him; he never felt confident. He did manage to go to work, but as soon as he got home, he continued to drink heavily.

I learned a lot about my own worthiness because of him. I found out shortly after we moved in together that Joel had fathered a child. Although the relationship had been brief, he still took responsibility for his son, and he had regular contact with him. I thought this was a positive sign. Then one summer, his son came for an extended visit—and I realized that I was the only one taking care of his son. Joel showed no responsibility and just sat on the couch, drinking beers. *It was then that I had my defining moment. I knew that if Joel and I had children, I would have to be emotionally responsible for them. I essentially would be a single parent—much like my mom had been.*

I decided at that moment that I deserved more than that. We'd been together for six years, but I knew it was time for this to come to an end.

Joel did not go easily. He became extremely angry, basically throwing a tantrum. He ripped up all of the photographs we had of us together. And he pulled the heads off some roses I had in a vase in the living room. My goal had been to get married and have kids, but now he was acting like a kid. What was I doing with someone who behaved so childishly? That should have been my first clue.

After we broke up, my friends tried to set me up with new guys, but I began to notice that these guys were too much like Joel. I wondered if I somehow attracted this kind of man. I decided I should do some work on myself before I start dating again, and that's what I have been doing. I now realize it's better to be by myself than to hold on to a destructive relationship. And that's a good start.

ALENA

Alena is truly in touch with her innermost feelings and knows what she wants out of life. She ended her most recent relationship quite abruptly, but she was strong enough to do so without hesitation when she realized she'd made a mistake in judgment. Today, at age thirty, Alena is hoping to find "the one." She currently resides in Denver, Colorado, where she is employed as an occupational therapist.

My parents were introduced to each other at a mutual friends wedding. My mother was sixteen and my father was seven years older, when they met. They were married three years later and I was born shortly thereafter. My father was the typical Russian father, very controlling, always yelling, but has a huge heart. My mother was a hard worker and when she returned home, after working she basically would check out of being a mom and would watch TV or read. Although she checked out, I always knew that my mother loved me.

My family is Jewish and Russian, and although we are not very religious, finding and marrying a Russian Jewish man is extremely important to my family. I am something of a black sheep in my family because at age thirty, I am still single and childless. My parents are concerned that I might not ever marry. My parents have tried to set me up on dates, but I haven't met anyone who interests me. My parents say that I will never find anyone to marry because I am too picky. That hurts my feelings, because it's not true; I'm just interested in being able to relate to the man on an emotional and spiritual level. I am looking for my true soul mate.

My last relationship, which was very promising at first, almost destroyed my relationship with my parents. I had just started my job as an occupational therapist, and Hal was one of my first patients. I was instantly attracted to him! It was arranged that he would come in on a weekly basis—he'd been in a car accident and needed therapy to regain use of his left arm. Because we worked so closely together, we began to develop a friendship, and we both looked forward to his appointments each week. I struggled for a year with the fact that he was my patient, because I had such an attraction to him. We seemed to have had so much in common—he was even Jewish—but I wasn't sure how he felt about me, personally, because I couldn't read his signals. There was also the ethical side of it, with my being his therapist and knowing I shouldn't get involved with a patient.

I finally decided, though, that I was going to tell Hal how I felt. So during his appointment the next week, I told him that I was attracted to him and that I'd begun to have feelings for him that went beyond therapist/patient feelings. And I told him that he needed to find another therapist because I really couldn't treat him any more.

He stared at me in disbelief because he had been hiding his feelings toward me. We decided to go out for drinks so we could really talk. During that conversation, Hal said something to me that should have been a warning sign to me: He said that he was attracted to me, but he didn't think that he was good enough for me. I thought he just had low self-esteem, but later I discovered that he was hiding a very important detail from me. But at that moment, I told him that he absolutely was "good enough" for me.

On our first real date, Hal made reservations at an elegant Russian restaurant because he wanted to learn about me and my culture. That was one of the most romantic gestures anyone had bestowed upon me. We became serious about each other very quickly. We saw each other almost every free moment that we had. I quickly fell in love with this guy.

My parents kept asking when they were going to meet him, and so we arranged to go out to dinner with them. During dinner, I could tell that Hal was going out of his way to please my father, but my father was not reciprocating. Later on that evening, my father called me on the phone to tell me that he was going to disown me if I continued my relationship with Hal. His reason was that he didn't believe that Hal was Jewish. My father had believed that Hal was "faking" being Jewish, just so my parents would like him. I thought my father was being ridiculous, and I told him so.

At first, I wasn't even going to insult Hal by repeating my father's accusation, but because we had no secrets between us (or so I thought), I decided to tell Hal what my father had said. After all, he was my father, and I loved him, and I wanted him to be happy for the love I'd found in Hal.

My defining moment, when I knew that Hal was not the one, occurred when I told Hal what my father had said—and Hal admitted that my father was right. Hal said he was actually Muslim but had lied to me because he knew it was important that I date Jewish men.

I guess many women would had been flattered by a guy who pretended he was something he was not, just to get a date, but I considered it a form of deception—right up there with lying and being unfaithful. I decided to break it off with him.

It really was my choice. I had loved Hal but not enough to have my family disown me. Our relationship would only complicate my family situation. Still, if he had been honest with me in the beginning, maybe we could have somehow salvaged our relationship. But because he'd been dishonest, I couldn't continue my relationship with him.

Ending the relationship was very difficult for me. I sincerely missed him after we broke up. Our relationship came to an end before it truly blossomed. We never even had the chance to make love. In all honesty, I can say that Hal was the love of my life. It was the first time that I had ever felt love that strong and that intense.

I am a firm believer in loving hard, and if I get hurt, it's okay, because that just means that I'll get more love eventually. I am realizing that you have to open yourself and be vulnerable to love because if you already put up a preconceived wall, you will never allow for someone good to come into your life.

And in the meantime of waiting to find "Mr. Right", I have my single girlfriends that I go out with and I have that underlying faith and trust that I will meet the person that I am meant to be with for how ever long. I still have that inner peace and inner knowledge that I will one day find the right man for me. Even now, my parents still try to set me up with several Russian Jewish guys and since the break-up with Hal, I have been on close to fifty dates that were arranged by family members. But these dates have just been flops. Until my family is able to understand who I am they will continue to arrange these types of dates that are nothing more than a "guy" for a "girl" instead of a "soul" for a "soul".

ANGELIQUE

~

Angelique admits that she was so consumed by wanting to get married that she ignored the red flags that were waving at her. After dating the same man for twelve years, her marriage lasted just eighteen months. Now thirty-nine years old and happily single, Angelique is a hair-stylist in Miami, Florida.

I grew up in a violent household. My dad was a very controlling and abusive man, and my parents fought all the time. Most of the time they fought about my dad's numerous affairs, but they didn't really need a reason to fight. Because I was frequently exposed to a lot of violence as a child, I determined that I never wanted a life like that.

I started dating when I was seventeen—that's when I met Ian. I found him very attractive, and my mom liked him too, which was important to me. Ian's family, on the other hand, hated me. They were very concerned that I was taking their son away from them. It didn't stop Ian and me from dating, but it did make for some uncomfortable family events. Ian's family is Irish and mine is Hispanic, so that was a sore spot with his father. His dad would make racial slurs in front of me.

As Ian and I continued in the relationship, I always put him as my top priority. It didn't take long to realize, though, that Ian always puts me last in his life. I always did whatever he wanted to do when we went on dates, but he never did anything that I wanted to do.

This should have been a red flag in our relationship, but I was blinded by love.

Several years later—Ian was in his mid-twenties by this time—he was excited when his parents bought him his own house. They paid all the expenses for him, and his mom came daily to clean, do his laundry, and prepare his meals. He lived in the house with several of his friends, and it was like a frat house. So even though he was living outside of his parents' house, he didn't try to achieve any independence or adult responsibility. And at this same time, I was building my career and finding my own place to live. This should have been another red flag.

Still, I wanted to get married. Ian said he wouldn't get married until he was thirty, so I stayed with him, knowing that one day he'd propose.

By the time he finally proposed to me, we had been in a relationship for twelve years. I'd waited a long time, but his proposal was far from romantic—he asked me to reach into the glove box of his car. Inside was a small box. When I asked him what it was, all he said was, "It's your ring." I was taken aback by the perfunctory tone, and so I didn't say anything. Finally, he said, "I'm asking you to marry me." That was it. No celebration or excitement. Still, I said yes.

After we got married, I thought my role in life was to please Ian. I cooked five out of seven days, and I gave him sex five out of seven days. My mom had always told me that a woman's job was to cater to her man. I wanted to make Ian as happy as possible. And I was determined not to have the type of violent marriage my parents had. During our marriage we never fought, because I always agreed with him. We never had money issues, because we kept our finances separate.

Our marriage seemed okay at first, but that's probably because I was the one making all the effort. After a few months, though, Ian started to become someone I didn't even recognize. I found out he was taking steroids. He claimed it was legal, but I didn't believe him. Then I noticed that he became more aggressive and temperamental. He was becoming more physically fit, but his patience was becoming very short and his thoughts were often clouded. I begged him to stop the steroids, and I tried to get him to see the effects they had on him, but he wouldn't listen to me. Instead, he became verbally abusive. I was reaching the end of my rope.

My defining moment came several months later. We had gone to dinner, and when we got home, Ian simply announced that he was "not ready to be married" and that he did not want children.

His announcement might have been because his thoughts were clouded again because of the steroids, but I was devastated and began to cry hysterically. I felt used and betrayed, because as far as I was concerned, the purpose of having sex was mainly to have children. That was the beginning of the end for me.

I was the one who moved out of the house—it was his house that his parents had bought for him, and my name was never put on the deed—and I moved in with my brother to a basement apartment. This was devastating for me because I felt I had come so far, and now I was going backwards. My sense of self-worth was at an all-time low.

Then one morning, after days and weeks of crying, I said to myself, "You are killing yourself. Now, stop it!"

I wanted to make a fresh start, so I moved to a new neighborhood. I wanted to pretend that I'd started in a new world. Today, I have become stronger as a person, but my emotions are still fragile. My experience with Ian has made it difficult for me to trust people.

As time goes by, I am starting to reclaim my power. Women often are willing to do many things for love, and they often lose their own self-worth. I realize now, though, that I would rather be alone for the rest of my life than lose my self-worth again. Ian might have taken a piece of me, but my whole self belongs to me.

KIMBERLY

~

Kimberly traveled to another continent in her efforts to be a good wife, only to discover that her husband was just as emotionally detached from her in China as he had been in the United States—and she was even more isolated because she couldn't speak the language. After four years of marriage, she realized that she had to start thinking about what was right for her. Now thirty-five and divorced, Kimberly resides in Windham, Maine, where she owns a book shop.

---

*M*y father passed away shortly before his and my mother's fortieth wedding anniversary. Their relationship was an extremely close one. They truly balanced each other out and supported each other. I assumed that was how my own life was going to be—that I would marry a man who would take care of me, emotionally and financially. I thought that I would go to college and meet my husband—as my parents had met in the 1950's—and that when we got married, I would stay home with my children, just as my mom had done.

I met Richard at a trade show in St. Louis, Missouri. He was twenty-six and was working for his family's business in the advertising industry, and I was twenty-seven and working for my family's business in the marketing industry. He was a handsome guy and physically strong. We clicked instantly and began to date.

His physical attributes were very attractive, but it was the sense of security that I had when I just walked down the street with him that endeared him to me. I felt very safe with him, although physically more than emotionally. He was such a very convincing kind of guy.

Richard lived in Vermont, not too far from where I lived in Maine, so we did the long-distance thing at the beginning of our relationship, and then we ended up living together—that wasn't really a conscious decision. He just began to gradually bring his stuff over to my house until all of a sudden he was living there.

I suppose one of the first red flags that I should have seen was that while we were dating, I lost touch with my girlfriends because all my time was spent with Richard, and he didn't want to socialize with them. He never tried to be friends with my friends. He was very into his own pursuits, and he didn't have time for other people's lives. He didn't include me with his friends, either—his friends were his and his alone, and he ensured that I had nothing to do with them. Even then, Richard compartmentalized his life.

I also was a little concerned that Richard was somewhat of a risk-taker. He participated in sports like rock climbing and seemed to thrive on the danger. I suspected that he had a binge-drinking problem too. He was never violent, so I never felt as though I was in any physical danger when he drank, but it did seem like a serious health problem.

I suppose it was because he was such a risk-taker that he was always trying to push the envelope, and toward the end of our relationship I suspected that he was having an affair. I think he got a thrill from testing how far a relationship outside of our marriage could go. This was another red flag that I chose to ignore.

Richard had such a tremendous power and charisma and was so extremely persuasive that he could talk me into almost anything. He was a great manipulator and enjoyed calling all the shots. I guess I kept missing the red flags in our relationship because in spite of some of the negative issues that would come up with Richard, there were a lot of positives in our relationship. Richard was very romantic and affectionate, and he could be very thoughtful. One night I came home from work to a candlelit dinner of franks and beans, which I thought was so romantic. He had many positive attributes, and that is why it was easy for me to say yes when, after two years of dating, Richard proposed.

I wasn't at all apprehensive about getting married—I loved him—but I did feel as though I was somewhat obligated to get married. Because Richard and I had lived together for two years, I wondered what people would think if our relationship did not result in marriage.

Soon after we returned from our honeymoon in Africa, Richard informed me that he wanted to go to graduate school to study Chinese History. I later found out that his motivation for this was because it was a difficult subject, and he got a kick out of telling people that's what he was studying. Richard was a very bright guy and very capable, but he also enjoyed showing off by telling people about his major in Chinese history. The only issue I had with it was that we had to move—he chose to go to a school in California.

Richard was very persuasive, though, because I never gave a thought to leaving Maine. He kept saying that this would be our little adventure, and so I said good-bye to my family and friends and headed with my new husband to California. That's just how convincing Richard was.

Life was not fun for me in California. I got a job because Richard was going to school. Our lives seemed to become more and more separated. He really had his own set of school friends, and I was not privy to that circle. They were learning to speak a language that was totally unfamiliar to me, and they had an enormous amount of school work that they worked on together. Richard would often spend his nights studying with this group, while I was left at home by myself. I began to resent Richard and the life that he had forced on me. I began hoping that something bad would happen to him—I had begun to think that his having an accident was going to be my only way out, because I never, ever wanted to face a divorce. I know now that when a wife is wishing for something bad to happen to her husband, it is really time to leave that relationship.

As he became more and more involved with his school work, Richard and I grew farther and farther apart. As he got closer to graduating, however, he told me that he wanted to do his PhD in China, and I was completely blindsided by this announcement. I certainly had no desire to live in China. I felt trapped in this marriage, because I was too afraid to divorce him—I was concerned what people back home would think—so going with him to China seemed like the only alternative. He convinced me that it would be fun and that going to China would be one big adventure for us.

We moved to China, and once we got there, I quickly understood that he was going to be in school most of the time, and I was going to be at home alone—again—but this time, in China! I felt stupid, because our relationship was just as miserable for me here as it had been in California. There was nothing for me to do all day. Phoning home was too expensive, and I couldn't even watch TV, because all of the programs were in Chinese. He kept telling me that I wasn't trying hard enough to make the best of the situation and that I should try to learn Chinese, but I had no interest in that. This was all Richard's dream, not mine.

All my time in China basically was taken up with making Richard's life easier. He was struggling with a very difficult school program, and it was up to me to take care of him. I didn't see how much he was taking me for granted. Richard was spending so much time with his "study group" that after a few months, I began to suspect that studying Chinese was not all that Richard was doing. I had no proof that he was having an affair; all I knew was that I was alone in a foreign country while my husband was off doing his own thing. He seemed completely detached from me, and even worse, he didn't seem to care.

My defining moment came after he had again stayed out with his friends. When I confronted him about staying out all night, he tried to put the blame on me, saying that I was not trying hard enough to make this arrangement work.

That was the point at which I knew I'd had enough. I had done little else but try hard to make the arrangement work, but Richard didn't see any of that. I told him then that I was going home to Maine, and after I did, I felt an overwhelming sense of calm. I knew that I was doing the right thing in leaving a man who didn't support me emotionally and who took me for granted. I left China two days later.

I still had to face my family and friends, and that concerned me more than actually getting a divorce. As soon as the plane landed in Maine, I immediately had an appointment to see a therapist, because I knew that I was going to be in need of help and guidance in order to deal with this. My therapist immediately put me on an anti-depressive. I am fully aware of how Tom Cruise feels about anti-depressives, but I think they should be in our drinking water! I knew that without the aid of that medication, I would never have been able to face anyone in my sleepy little town in Maine.

I spent Thanksgiving with my family and by the time Christmas came and Richard had not followed me home, I knew for sure that our marriage was over. And it was and I prepared myself and began to slowly tell everyone that I would be divorcing.

As for the people in my town—everyone was extremely supportive and kind to me. It was a huge relief for me to be around people who were connecting with me, emotionally. In fact two of my mothers friends who were well in their sixties were sitting on my mother's porch one morning talking about how neither of them had felt that their husbands were "the ones". In fact one of these women admitted that she knew she had made a mistake while she was on her honeymoon! Once I began to share with everyone about my intentions to divorce Richard, it began to open a floodgate of stories from the town's women. After I started hearing the older women talking about how brave I was to get out of something that wasn't working for me and how they wished that they had done the same thing, I realized that most of the people in my town, were unfortunately unhappy with their relationships and that they wished that they could do something about it. I realized that life is too short for anyone to stay in situations that don't make them feel good. For as much as I thought I was a Jezebel for getting a divorce, I can only imagine how emotionally difficult it was for these women who were hanging onto their bad marriages all these years in a quiet desperation. These women felt as though divorce was not an option for them. And with the love and support of the townspeople, I've realized that my divorce is not a negative reflection on me and that I am still a good person.

The funny thing is that both of those sixty year old women that I spend time with rocking away on my mother's porch are now divorced. In fact several other women in my town have joined the divorcee club as well. I believed that I may have started a trend in my quiet little town in Maine.

JENNIFER

~

Jennifer learned at an early age that she could only rely on herself. When she met the man who would become her first husband, she happily let him take over the responsibility of making all the decisions—it was a relief to rely on someone else for a change. It wasn't long, though, before she realized that she was allowing him to control her every move. It was only after she left the marriage that she was able to find herself again. Now fifty-six years old and remarried, Jennifer enjoys life with her husband and grown sons in Stamford, Connecticut, where she owns and operates a conceirge service.

---

*M*y parents were alcoholics who always argued about who drank more. I was the second oldest of four daughters, and life was very difficult for my sisters and me because even as young children, we knew couldn't rely on either of our parents. My older sister and I essentially raised and mothered our two younger sisters. As a result of my up bringing, I became increasingly self-reliant.

I met Jack at a youth convention when I was seventeen. He was gregarious, self-confident, and extremely handsome. We learned that we lived about an hour apart, and because we hit it off so well at the convention, we started getting together every other weekend. I continued to see Jack during my senior year of high school, but our parents did not want us to go to college together. I suppose they wanted us to spend time apart to see if we really cared about each other, but we felt that we'd spent our entire senior year apart because we lived in different towns. Eventually, our parents agreed that Jack and I could attend the same college. We were very serious about college and were very goal-oriented.

In our junior year, Jack went to my father to discuss proposing to me. I think I did love Jack at that time, and I felt that he loved me, but I wasn't particularly excited about planning a wedding. It became much more of an event to satisfy my parents.

Because we were both still in school, we didn't have a honeymoon. After spending our wedding night in a hotel, we moved into our apartment. I did get excited about fixing up our own place and entertaining friends. We enjoyed socializing as a couple, and we also enjoyed our time alone together. Our marriage seemed to really be working for us. It would have been okay with me if things had continued this way for several years, but Jack a "let's look ahead" kind of person; he was the one who suggested we should have a baby. I wasn't sure it was a good idea, but I agreed with him. I was unable to see that he was being controlling at this time; I just thought he was being attentive to me and wanted to make a good life for us.

I usually let Jack make the decisions in our marriage; I never really argued. After coming from life with my chaotic parents, being married to Jack was a much more stable and quiet life. And I felt our life was so organized because of him. When I was growing up in an alcoholic household, everything had been in flux, and my parents were slobs. I was always disgusted by their cigarette butts, so I was always cleaning. So it was really very nice to have control of my environment, and I was happy to have a clean home.

I got pregnant at age twenty-one. Our son was born the year before we both graduated from college, so finances were tight. By the time our son was almost a year old, Jack made his career choice: He was going to work for the state police.

I'd like to say things got even better for us and our family once Jack started his job, but his behavior changed after he joined the state troopers. It was not immediately apparent, but there were subtle signs. He would come home and tell me how the other state troopers were treating people negatively—it wasn't physical abuse, but they'd be rude and disrespectful. It wasn't long before Jack started treating me the same way. I had to remind him that he wasn't arresting me; I was his wife.

Within a year I was pregnant again. Jack was transferred during my eighth month of pregnancy, and so we had to move. When our second son was born, Jack was working long hours, and I felt stressed and very isolated. It was a cold winter, and I was stuck in the house with two young children. Jack was ignoring me much of the time when he was home; he treated me more like a possession than a partner—I was good for his image when we were out in public or at a work-related event. With me on his arm, he could present the picture of the happily married man. More and more, there was a distance between us, but we continued in our marriage for several more years.

My defining moment came when Jack insisted I go with him to a party—he wanted to present the married image—but then he spent all his time talking to other people. I realized that he didn't want to spend time with me. And I also realized that if he didn't want to spend time with me now, he certainly wouldn't want to grow old with me.

Soon after that night, I told Jack that I was leaving him, and by this time, he didn't seem to care. Maybe I was naïve, but it never occurred to me that he might be having an affair. I later found out that he had been cheating on me with the co-chairman of our son's Little League team. At the time, however, I suppose I closed my eyes to those signs, because I wanted to give my sons a better family life than I'd had. So my leaving him just made it easier for him to be with Bev. It was a crushing blow to me when my sons decided to live with Jack and Bev when they were teenagers, but I guess boys need their father.

After the divorce, I developed a new self-confidence. I was happy to have my own place, too, and when I came home from work it would look the same way it had when I left it. I grew to relish living alone; I was able to travel for work and became president of my professional organization. While I was married, Jack made me feel so guilty about doing anything for myself. After the divorce, I could do what I wanted to do, without having to answer to someone.

I eventually decided that I was ready to share my life again, and I remarried. I've been with my husband for fifteen wonderful years, and he's shown me that a relationship can be on equal terms if it's based, as ours is, on openness and honesty..

PATTI

~

Patti rode an emotional roller coaster for several years with her then-husband before she was able to get off the ride. She freely admits that finally calling a halt to his game-playing was one of the best decisions she ever made. Now, the forty-two-year-old dentist is a newlywed, having remarried seven years after her divorce. She and her husband live in Tucson, Arizona.

———————————

*E*ven as a child, I knew that I never wanted to duplicate my parents' relationship when I grew up. My father was a rather difficult, very controlling man, who expected other people to do whatever he wanted. Over the years, my mom made a lot of concessions for my father, and I knew that I didn't want to do that in any of my relationships with men.

My father always told me to give one hundred percent and expect zero in return. This was drilled into my head, and it applied to everything, whether it was school work, a job, or a boyfriend. It made me very cautious about men, and although I began dating in my teens, I waited a long time to get married because I wanted to be absolutely certain that I was choosing the right one.

I met Kevin while I was in dental school—he was two years behind me—and at first, I didn't like him at all. He seemed too arrogant and was quite a flirt. He was persistent, though, in trying to win me over, so eventually, I gave in and agreed to go out with him. After the first date, we began going out together on a regular basis.

I learned that Kevin was very attentive, and he seemed like he had a good head on his shoulders. Even though I was ahead of him in school, he was seven years my senior. I tend to fall for older men, though, so his age was not a concern. He'd been married and had a twelve-year-old son, but that wasn't a concern either. In fact, the way he interacted with his son showed me that he was a good father. Kevin also was an excellent cook, and at the beginning of our relationship, he was always trying to impress me with his culinary skills.

We had a whirlwind courtship, getting engaged just four months after we started dating. Our relationship just instantly felt right, and so we didn't waste any time. We were married six months after getting engaged, just after my graduation.

When we came back from our honeymoon, we moved in with his mother, who was living in a big house out in the country. I was not yet working because it took me six months to find a job, so I would be at home all day with his mother while Kevin was at school. But it didn't matter what time of day he finished his classes; he would never come home until at least seven o'clock at night. As a newlywed, I expected that he'd want to rush home to see me, so the fact that he was hanging out on campus instead of coming home was quite hurtful to me. When I confronted him about this, however, he told me to get used to it, because the honeymoon was over. In fact, he'd tell me that quite often. Whenever I mentioned any problems or concerns, instead of talking with me to find a solution, he'd just say, "The honeymoon is over. Get used to it."

We lived with his mother for six months, and then, after I joined a dental practice, we bought our first home. Kevin continued to go to school and enjoy himself with his friends. I didn't mind his socializing, but I did start to resent that while I was working all day, Kevin did nothing in his free time but hang out. I became aware of the fact that there were two distinctive sides to Kevin. One was charming and liked to cook for me and didn't mind helping out, but the other didn't want to do anything—and this one had been showing up more frequently.

I was doing everything in our marriage. I was earning the money, doing all the grocery shopping, cooking all the meals (his cooking for me came to an abrupt end as soon as we got married), cleaning the house, doing the laundry, and taking care of the yard work. I was exhausted. I would get home at seven o'clock to find Kevin watching television—if he was there at all.

I tried to talk to him about how I felt, and he'd promise to try to help out more. But nothing changed. He was just turning into a blob, and I was getting more and more overwhelmed. Things were quickly going from bad to worse.

Because I grew up in a Catholic household, I always found solace and peace whenever I attended church. So I started going to a nearby church to try to figure out my life. Kevin and I have only been married for a little over a year, and I didn't think that we should be having so many problems. We just couldn't communicate—every time we talked, it turned into an argument. Eventually, I asked Kevin if he would go to counseling with me, but although he kept promising that he would go, he never followed through. That was an indication to me that he really wasn't committed to making our marriage work. In fact, that was an indication to me that he was not interested in our relationship at all.

The old Kevin—the one that I had dated and fallen in love with—no longer existed. I just couldn't understand what was making his personality change so drastically. It was like he was one man before marriage and a completely different man after marriage. I wondered if the only reason he married me was because he wanted me to take care of him.

All the stress of trying to deal with Kevin and our constant arguments took a toll on my health—he was literally making me sick. I had a persistent feeling of ill health. At one point, I was diagnosed with laryngitis, bronchitis, a sinus infection, and conjunctivitis, all at the same time. I was prescribed strong antibiotics and told to rest. I dragged myself home from the doctor's, but although I was clearly quite ill, Kevin never asked how I was feeling.

My defining moment came as I crawled into bed, so sick and exhausted that I could barely move, and Kevin bounced down on the bed next to me and said he needed a massage—would I rub his shoulders for him?

I couldn't believe how inconsiderate and unfeeling he was. All he wanted was for me to cater to his needs, while he ignored my needs. That action really drew the line in the sand for me. This incident proved to me that he was incapable of being there for me, and I could never count on him when the chips were down. Kevin showed me that he truly was a narcissistic person, and there was no room in his world for anyone else, including a wife.

When I recovered from my illnesses, I confronted Kevin and told him that he had to leave. It took him about two hours to pack and get out of my life.

Now my life is back on track. Currently, I have a thriving dental practice, and seven months ago, I married a wonderful man, who was able to show me that two people can share a lasting love.

KAYLA

~

Kayla's history of abuse led her to marry a man who was much like her father—violent, demanding, and abusive. She fortunately was able to end that relationship, but then she became involved with someone whose deceit was another form of abuse. Now forty-eight years old and divorced, she specializes in helping abuse victims. Kayla currently resides in Buckhead, Atlanta. She is an attorney who specializes in matrimonial law in fact she handled her own divorce.

---

*M*y mom and dad were from Greece, and so they had some Old World ideas about raising children. My dad's idea of discipline was to beat my siblings and me with a strap. He was only doing to us kids what his father had done to him. My mom never tried to stop him when he came after us—often punching us or pulling our hair—and so I learned never to trust my mom or dad.

When I was a teenager, my dad would never let me go on dates. I eventually found out the reason for this: He had already arranged a marriage for me—it was his way of thanking the man who had gotten my dad into the construction union. And I was supposed to just go along with it; I was around eighteen at the time, and it was entirely too much for me to cope with. I knew somehow I needed to escape from this situation. My dad was unrelenting, telling me I had no choice. But one night, I quietly packed up all my belongings, put everything in my little brother's wagon, and walked to my friend Sue's house. Her parents took me in and let me stay in their basement. Later on, I would marry Sue's brother, Parker.

I got pregnant just a few months after marrying Parker. I remember that I made a candlelight dinner for him, hoping to make it a memorable evening. But Parker came home drunk after spending many hours out with his friends. He started ranting—I don't even remember anymore what it was about—and before I knew it, I was on the floor. He then went to the kitchen cabinets, took out the canned goods, and started pelting me with them. Then he ripped the phone out of the wall before he passed out on the kitchen floor.

His abuse escalated during my pregnancy. When I was seven months pregnant, he threw me down an entire flight of stairs. Before I could get away, he beat my head on the floor and against the radiator. I was able to escape from the house and went to my friend's house. She called the police and took me to the hospital. I never returned to Parker; I filed for divorce.

By this time, I felt I had no identity, and I had to learn to find myself. I worked multiple jobs to make ends meet, and I focused my attention on raising my daughter, who was born shortly after I divorced Parker.

I met Bryce through some mutual friends. He was tall and blond, with blue eyes, a warm smile, and fabulous dimples. He was fun-loving and joyful. He worked as a stock broker and seemed to be financially established. Within four months of our meeting, he moved in with me. We got married just one month later.

I was taking college classes at this time, and everything appeared to be going well. We didn't go out much, but that was okay with me. Bryce said he wanted to be a family man; he wanted to be very involved with raising my daughter, so we stayed home most nights.

Before long, however, Bryce began to drink heavily. He started drinking on the commuter train at night, so by the time he arrived home, he was often intoxicated. His personality changed completely; he seemed depressed more often than not. I could not deal with his sudden change, and I wondered why he was not happy with me. (Of course, I took responsibility for his unhappiness, assuming that I was doing something to provoke his depression.) But I didn't understand what was really going on, and I didn't know how much longer I could take it.

His parents threw a party for us to celebrate our first anniversary. I found out later, though, that his mother's intention was to tell me about the "real Bryce."

My defining moment came when I found out that Bryce had been—and still was—living a lie. Everything he had told me about himself was untrue. I could not accept such deceit—it truly was almost as if he'd slapped me.

His mother told me that he had lied about where he'd gone to school, where he worked, how much money he made—he'd even lied about loving me so that I would marry him. I felt completely betrayed, but the final straw was when I confronted Bryce, and he just shrugged and flashed his affable smile, as if he'd just told me a good joke.

Although I was so desperate to provide a good father figure for my daughter and to appear as if we had a normal family, I couldn't take it anymore. I told Bryce I was filing for divorce and that he had two days to move out of my apartment.

Today, I am an attorney who specializes in marital issues. I help women with a history of abusive relationships understand that they are not alone. I help them work on regaining their self-confidence so that they can leave any abusive situation. And I try to empower them so that they can make decisions for themselves once again.

YUMI

~

Yumi is a thirty-year-old, self-proclaimed sex addict. She acknowledges that she leads a promiscuous lifestyle that often hampers her from developing meaningful relationships. She recently ended a long-term relationship because she and her partner had different sexual needs. Yumi lives in the Soho area of New York City, where she works in a bookstore.

I love to have sex. I think I may have a sexual addiction, but I've never been officially diagnosed. It could be that I'm simply a creature of my environment.

My grandmother was from China and was very subservient to my grandfather. I also saw my mother take a subservient role to my stepfather, who was abusive and domineering. As I started dating, I found myself mirroring the roles my mother and grandmother played, and I was very subservient to many of my boyfriends.

My parents had allowed me to have a boyfriend when I turned sixteen years old. My mother decided to have a heart-to-heart talk with me at this time, warning me about the dangers of having sex. It was during this talk that she revealed to me that she was speaking from personal experience—the man that I'd grown up thinking was my father was really my stepfather; my real father was the boy who'd gotten my mother pregnant as a teenager. I felt betrayed when I heard the truth, but in a way, I was relieved to learn my mother's husband was not my biological father—he had been sexually molesting me ever since I was twelve. I think that my mother knew that her husband was abusing me, but she never did anything about it.

Even prior to being sexually molested, I was preoccupied by sexual thoughts—this was before I was eight years old. I began to masturbate at a very young age, and I knew all about sex before I'd even turned five. My stepfather would always leave his pornography videos and magazines where I could find them, and I enjoyed looking at them. I see now how my adult relationships with men have suffered as a result of my childhood obsession with sex. I tend to allow the relationships to become sexual very quickly. I've never been without a man since I started dating, and before I leave one boyfriend, I always have another man waiting in the wings. Somewhere I heard that a woman should be alone and go through all four seasons before beginning another relationship. I wish that I could somehow do that. But I think that I am too afraid to be alone. I also think that I am looking for validation through my relationships.

Because of my abusive relationship with my stepfather, I treated most of the men in my life like crap. Subsequently, I've thrown away a lot of good men. But I met my match when I met Toby. I was twenty-four years old and was working part-time in a music shop while attending graduate school; Toby worked there, too.

One day he asked me to attend a poetry open-mike event at a local café. Once we got to the café, I realized that Toby was going to read some of his own poetry. His writing was beautiful, and the audience enjoyed his readings as well. As the days went on, I became even more attracted to him because of his creativity and talents. Although he wasn't handsome in the traditional sense, his ability to write such beautiful and sensual poetry was very appealing to me.

My parents weren't too happy that I was dating him because Toby was African American, and my family is Chinese. My parents didn't mind if I had black friends, but to become romantically involved with a black man was totally taboo.

Although Toby's family liked me, they also really loved his ex-girl-friend. At times, they would accidentally call me by his ex-girl-friend's name. Everyone would always apologize for doing so, but I wondered if Toby was still somehow involved with her.

At this point in our relationship, I was in love with Toby. I needed to know if I should continue to invest in this relationship and risk damaging my good relationship with my parents. So I had a serious talk with Toby. I told him that I expected him to be loyal and completely honest with me. I said that I would prefer that he tell me if he found himself attracted to someone else, because I could easily let go.

After dating for close to a year, Toby told me that he actually was becoming attracted to his ex-girlfriend again. I kept my word and allowed him to explore that possibility. I didn't even have any animosity toward him because at least he was honest. We were apart for almost two years, but then Toby and I decided that we were really in love with each other, and we wanted to give our relationship another try. My parents were not happy with the news that Toby and I would be seeing one another again. In fact, they said it was best if I didn't live at home any longer. So Toby and I decided to move in together.

Ours was such a deep and loving relationship that I was sure that Toby was the "one." Neither one of us could envision ourselves in relationships with other people. And within a couple of months, we discovered that I was pregnant. Toby was very happy and supportive during the pregnancy—although it was quite short; I miscarried at three months. I became pregnant three more times, but each one ended in miscarriage. It was a very sad time for us, but we came through it together.

I knew that Toby loved me because he was willing to do almost anything for me. There was a time in my life that I wondered if I was bisexual. I wanted to experiment, and Toby was very understanding of my needs. I was attracted to a particular girl, and I often envisioned her in the bedroom with Toby and me. I told Toby about my thoughts and suggested a threesome, but he was adamant about the fact that he was not interested. Finally, after a year and a half, he agreed to do it. I enjoyed it so much that I wanted her to be a frequent guest in our bedroom, but Toby never wanted to do it again. I wasn't too happy about his decision because I was always looking for ways to spice up things in the bedroom.

But I was beginning to notice that Toby just couldn't keep up with me, sexually. I craved sex almost all of the time, but once a week—or less—was enough for him. We would argue over this constantly. This was how all of my relationships had been. I would be the one that would always want sex, and the guy just didn't have the same level of desire. I would feel frustrated and rejected and wonder why they didn't desire me as much as I desired them.

When we'd been together about eight years, Toby was performing more often in clubs—he'd become quite talented at writing rap music—and he'd stay out quite late. I suspected that he was staying out late because he found someone else.

Our sex life was at an all-time low by this time. He said that my needs ("demands," as he put it) were too much for him. He felt like sex was all I thought about, and he was beginning to feel like less of a man because he couldn't fulfill my desires. I couldn't even defend myself, because everything he said was basically true. Still, we'd had sex quite frequently at the beginning of our relationship, and I couldn't figure out what had changed.

About a month later, a woman called our apartment, asking for Toby. *My defining moment, when I realized Toby was not the "one," came as this woman proceeded to tell me that I was putting too much sexual pressure on Toby—and I realized he'd been sharing intimate details of our life together with her.*

When I confronted him, he said that he had to share how he was feeling with someone else, because I wasn't listening to him. I thought he was cheating on me with this woman, but as it turned out, he really was just confiding in her. Still, I didn't like being talked about to a stranger, especially about our private sex life. I realized it was time to cut Toby loose. So after eight years of dating, I chose to end the relationship.

Currently, I am dating a guy I knew in high school. We had lost touch with each other for ten years and recently reconnected. So far, he's been able to keep up with my desires. I know that everyone has a different level of desire, but I hope that this is the man who is compatible with my level.

I've discovered something that is quite the rage in New York City—they're called "cuddle parties" and I attend one frequently. It's a chance for people, who in most cases don't even know one another, and opportunity to cuddle. I find that it's a wonderful experience to be able to feel someone next to me. They are so wildly popular that you can find one in full swing, almost every night of the week.

Recently, I participated in a twenty-one day no-sex strike. But by the time I was in the third day I masturbated and by the sixth day I went out and had full-blown sex. I know that everyone has different levels of desire, but I just wish I could meet a man that was compatible with my level of desire.

STEFANIA

~

Stefania grew up observing her parents' warm and loving relationship. She naturally assumed that she eventually would have the same sort of relationship with a man. Unfortunately, she became involved with someone who abused her. Now forty-one years old, she is proud of the fact that she was able to stand up to him and walk away. Stefania lives in Santa Monica, California, where she is an accountant.

---

*M*y parents emigrated from Cuba to avoid Communism. They remember the Castro regime, and it wasn't pretty. So when my parents were able to leave Cuba, they packed a few personal items and left the rest of their old lives behind. They made a house filled with love for me and my older sister. My parents they have definitely had their ups and downs but they were always resilient, and I really feel they loved each other.

Because I saw the loving marriage my parents had as I was growing up, I hoped to duplicate it to some degree. I was hopeful that I would find someone who was loving and kind and who would take care of me. I soon met Gilberto.

Gilberto was twenty-one and very handsome, with his dark hair and blue eyes. There was something about him, though, that made him seem vulnerable, and I was intrigued by this. Gilberto was a construction worker, and I had some negative stereotypes of construction workers; I had doubts that I should date him. But he seemed so genuinely interested in me and our chemistry was so strong that I couldn't refuse his request for a date.

Initially, Gilberto and I enjoyed our time together. We developed an incredible bond, and we tried to spend all our time together. We would go to the movies and out for pizza; he was constantly on my mind. I truly felt that I loved him and that he loved me.

Even when Gilberto became very possessive, I thought it showed that he loved me. He began to dictate what clothes I could wear, where I could go, and who I could see. After a few months, we began a sexual relationship, which was the first one for me. I felt especially bonded to him then; he seemed to have a mesmerizing effect on me.

But it didn't take long for Gilberto to exhibit further issues. One day, for no apparent reason, he slapped me across the face. I was shocked! When I asked why he'd done that, he slapped me again.

Soon, everything began to crumble. The slapping was bad enough, but soon he began kicking me and punching me. He was a foot taller than I was and outweighed me at least 150 pounds, so there was no way that I could fight him. He punched me so hard in my jaw that it was completely black and blue. One day, when we were visiting his family's summer home, Gilberto even pulled a gun on me. It was a hand gun that his father used for hunting quail. Gilberto looked at me with no expression and said, "If I pull this trigger, what do you think will happen? Will you run, or will you just fall?" I screamed, which fortunately his father heard. I don't know what might have happened if his father hadn't been there.

I was ashamed that my first relationship was with such a volatile guy. At this point we had been together for three years. He was such a controlling and manipulative person that I can't believe I stayed with him as long as I did. I suppose I was the typical abused woman—I still loved him, and that's why I continued to stay with him.

My defining moment actually came in a dream. I dreamed that I had children with Gilberto, and he attacked the kids. I tried to protect my kids in the dream by shouting "Wake up!"

And that was my personal awakening. I finally realized that I had to break away from him. I told Gilberto that I was not going to see him anymore. My dream convinced me that it was time to take some action. And that's just what I did. As for Gilberto, he was hit by a truck, developed tuberculosis and his dad just recently informed me that it would be wise for me to have an AIDS test performed.

DANA

Dana tried for years to follow the traditional roadmap for a relationship, but she found it was covered in too many potholes. After suffering through two abusive marriages, she listened to her heart and followed the road less taken. Today, Dana is happily involved with a woman who is her true soul mate. Now fifty years old, Dana and her two beautiful children live with her partner in St. Louis, Missouri, where she works in an advertising agency.

---

*W*hen I was eight years old, my daddy attempted to stab my mother to death, right in front of me. I'll never forget the look on her face as the knife was plunged into her chest and all of the blood came spurting out from her. I never understood why he was never punished for the things he did. My mother would always take him back. In addition to him being a physical abuser, my father was also a cheat. He actually had been seeing a woman across town, whom he produced two children with. My mother was fully aware of this other woman and family. In fact my mother would baby-sit those children at times so that my father and this other woman could go out on dates. As I was growing up, I realized that when my father would disappear for months at a time, it was because he was living in the other household. He spent all of my childhood alternating between the two homes.

My mother obviously was a very tolerant woman, probably more tolerant than most. I know that I would never put up with half of what she put up with from my father. Of course, watching the way my father treated her had an impact on how I would act in my own relationships. I was determined to never let a man make me look foolish, and I would not tolerate a man who hit or cheated on me.

I always felt a little bit different from the other girls when I was growing up. My girlfriends seemed to be concerned about how attractive they were to guys, but I just didn't care about that. In fact, ever since I was young, I found myself more attracted to girls. I loved the smell of women, and I always wanted to touch them. I found the curves of a woman's body to be much more exciting than the straight up and down of a man's body.

When I was around ten years old, I became more curious about seeing a woman's unclothed body. I remember how excited I was that one of my friends had started to grow pubic hair, and she asked if I wanted to see. From that moment on, I knew that I was meant to be in a relationship with a woman.

I never understood, though, what was wrong with a girl liking girls. I would tell my mother and my sister about my desires, and because they had such a negative reaction to my feelings, I quickly learned to keep my desires to myself.

I struggled with my sexuality in high school, so much so that I decided to have a heart-to-heart talk with my mother. She convinced me that I was *not* gay and that I was just caught in the current turmoil of the 1960s. So again, I went back into the closet.

When I was seventeen years old, I decided to try the traditional way of dating, because that was expected of me. I began to date a guy name Teddy, who lived in my neighborhood. I didn't particularly enjoy dating him, but I was willing to do what was expected of me. Teddy was nice enough, but I didn't feel any major attraction to him. In fact, the only reason I continued to go out with him was because I was curious about what everyone was talking about when they talked about "doing it."

I soon found out. Teddy and I had sex and continued "doing it" until I discovered that, at the age of twenty, I was pregnant. I was always against having a child out of wedlock, so although neither one of us wanted to, we got married. Predictably, this turned out to be a major mistake, especially because Teddy became physically abusive. I had always promised myself, ever since I was a child, that hitting was the one thing that I would not tolerate from a man. Teddy had been a good father to our children—we had two in five years—but I couldn't stay with him and take his physical abuse.

I did want to give my children a "normal" home life, though, so I hoped to eventually meet someone else. I was in the closet and kept denying my true attraction. Seven years after my divorce from Teddy, I met Alec, and I decided to give marriage another try. I wasn't attracted to him, but I did think he was a nice guy—until our wedding night. Alec usually was a pretty mellow guy, but that night, we got into an argument, and he hit me.

That was my defining moment—but it wasn't that I knew Alex wasn't the "one"; it was that I knew that no guy could ever be the one. That was the end of my being in a relationship with men.

I have since embraced my sexuality, officially. Currently, I am in a very loving relationship with a woman. It is not perfect, but it is definitely a happier relationship than those I had with men. For the first time, I am in a relationship with someone who communicates with me, rather than hitting. Even the sex is better, because it is gentler with a woman.

Some people have not accepted my decision to come out of the closet, but most of my old friends—those who knew me prior to my coming out—are still my friends today. I guess I got what I needed from a man—my two beautiful children. Life is good.

MAUREEN

~

Maureen wanted a relationship like her parents had—maybe it wouldn't be perfect, but she and her partner would handle the good and the bad together, because they would have made a commitment to each other. It was difficult for Maureen to follow through on such a commitment, however, when the partner she chose became abusive. Today, at age twenty-five, Maureen has taken back her power. Currently single, she lives in New York, where she is a professional boxer. She has won many professional bouts and was recently Hilary Swank's main sparring partner in the Academy Award winning movie "Million Dollar Baby."

———————

You've heard the phrase "solid as a rock"? That is how I would describe my parents' marriage. They met when my mom was sixteen years old and my dad was nineteen. They dated for seven years and were madly in love. Even their priest was aware of their devotion to one another so one day he told my dad, "You've got to marry that woman," So, being the good Irish-Catholic that he was, my dad did what he was told and willingly married my mom. Five years later my brother was born. And ten years later, I was born.

My mom likes to tell the story of how I kicked and moved around when she was pregnant with me—I was a real fireball, even before I was born. As a newborn, I was able to hold up my head and look around the hospital nursery.

My dad was a New York City police detective and former Marine, so he was strict and raised us on a military-precision schedule. I believed that rigorous discipline helped me to be extremely disciplined in my adult life. My mom was the sympathetic, understanding peacemaker in the family. Because my dad loved my mom, he would always give in to her when they disagreed. This is one of the secrets to their successful forty-year marriage. They were also strong believers in following through with their marriage vows to be together forever. They made the commitment to stick together until the end. This made an impression on me, and it was what sometimes led me to stay in relationships that I should have left.

At the time I became interested in boys, my parents hadn't told me about sex; I learned about the birds and the bees from my friends. I was always very selective in choosing a boyfriend. I secretly was looking for a relationship like my parents had, so I always looked for the good in every boy I dated.

I was sixteen when I met Lorenzo—he was twenty. He was tall, had black hair, and was attractive. I was looking for a guy who could protect me and make me feel safe, and Lorenzo seemed to fit that profile. Protection had always been a big deal for me. So when Lorenzo strutted into my life with an air of confidence and a swagger in his step, I knew I'd found my protector.

We started out as friends, because for me to have sex, I have to be able to feel an emotional connection to the person, and so we continued as only friends. But when I turned eighteen, the sky was the limit. And so we began our sexual relationship. We did not start off hot and heavy because living in this day and time you have to be careful, so I asked him to take an AIDS test, and he did so. He even brought the printed proof that he had a clean bill of health. I didn't know it at the time, but he really took that test for employment reasons and not to please me. Lorenzo wasn't particularly romantic, but that was not important to me. We spent our time together at the park or at each other's homes. I can still remember the first red flag that waved in our relationship, although I ignored it at the time. We were in bed together, he started asking me about my sexual experiences—how old was the oldest guy I kissed, how many partners had I had—and I could not understand where this was coming from. He became irate when he learned I wasn't a virgin—and then he proceeded to tell me that he had slept with my best friend. I was shocked and appalled because I could not understand why he was telling me this, right after we'd made love.

I should have gotten up from that bed and left him, but instead, I calmed him down, and we continued our relationship. Soon, however, everything began to turn really ugly.

One day I was at work, and I asked Lorenzo if he would go to my house and bring a couple of CDs to me. My dad was home, so he just directed Lorenzo to my room, telling him where to find my CD collection. But once he was in my room, Lorenzo went through my drawers and found a notebook, in which I kept a list of guys I'd liked. Lorenzo was sure it was a list of guys I'd had sex with, and he was furious. He came to my workplace, and I could tell from the angry scowl on his face that something was wrong. He threw the notebook at me and said, "What's all this? All the men you have had sex with?"

I tried to explain to him about the list and that I was only interested in being with him. I wanted to maintain our relationship, even though he was being irrational, because I wanted to emulate the type of loyalty my parents had in their marriage. I was planning to stay with Lorenzo at all costs, but I had no idea what that cost would be.

He became angry with me, more and more often, until one day he suddenly struck me—actually hit me across the face. He slapped me so hard that my ears where ringing. This sudden change of his behavior came out of nowhere! How could a man who was once so sweet turn so evil? Where was his anger coming from?

I began to think that I was doing something to agitate him. I tried to figure out what I was doing to make him so angry. I didn't understand at the time that he had his own issues, and none of this was my fault. Instead, I blamed myself and protected him. Even though the physical and emotional abuse continued for some time, I never let anyone know that he was harming me. He punched me in my face so hard on one occasion that I had to have eight stitches, but I pretended that it was a sports injury.

And yet I wanted to be loved and protected so much that I stayed with him—until the day I finally saw that I couldn't continue any longer; it wasn't any one incident that triggered it. *My defining moment came when I suddenly saw that because of Lorenzo, I was starting to lose my identity. I didn't know who or what I was. It was now time for me to take back my power and start protecting myself.*

And so I left him. I finally and definitely left him—and boy, how invigorated I felt. Breaking up with Lorenzo was the most empowering moment of my life. It was then that I decided to protect myself and not play the victim ever again. I was always athletic, and so I decided to take up the sport of boxing. Since boxing is a sport that's about discipline, skill, and perseverance, I knew I already had those qualities inside of me, but while I was stuck in my relationship with Lorenzo, I didn't tap into those resources. I've been boxing ever since and have sought to be the best boxer that I could be. I started boxing in the amateur division and the Golden Gloves, and now I am boxing at the professional level.

I know the power of my hands, but I would never misuse my power, as Lorenzo did. Now, however, I protect myself. I don't need someone to protect me. I can do it myself. Watch out, world! Here I come.

ABOUT THE AUTHORS

JUDY BOLTON is a psychotherapist and specializes in family and marital issues. She is a graduate of Columbia University. She has appeared in Newsday and numerous newspapers and has appeared on television and radio programs including; the Rachael Ray show, *CBS News and Montel Williams*. She is a contributing writer for Lifetimetv.com and YahooPersonals.com and serves as spokesperson for Yahoo! National Break-up Season. She is also the founder of *Dreams For A Day*, an organization which makes dreams come true for terminally ill adults. Judy currently resides in Long Island, New York with her two sons.

WENDY BOLTON FLOYD is a contributing writer for Lifetimetv.com and YahooPersonals.com and serves as spokesperson for Yahoo! National Break-up Season. She has appeared on the Rachael Ray show and countless news programs across the country and has been a guest on several radio shows. She has been featured in the The Orlando Sentinel and other major newspapers. Wendy holds a M.A. degree from the New York City University, Queens College and currently resides in Long Island, New York with her husband and children.

If interested in having Judy and Wendy for book club participation and other events, please contact us at www.whendidyouknow.org

978-0-595-41146-7
0-595-41146-0

Printed in the United States
82203LV00005B/67

9 780595 411467